WHO IS LIKE THE LORD?

WHO IS LIKE THE LORD?

EXPLORING THE ATTRIBUTES OF GOD

DR. DEWAYNE BRYANT

ISBN-10: 1944704264
ISBN-13: 978-1944704261

Library of Congress Control Number: 2016937492

Published by Start2Finish
Fort Worth, Texas 76244
www.start2finish.org

Printed in the United States of America

Cover Design: Josh Feit, Evangela.com

To Bobby and Shannon Davis

The best adopted grandparents our
five little girls could have ever wanted.

CONTENTS

UNDERSTANDING GOD

Who is God? An easy way to figure out what you think about him is to imagine what he looks like. How we think of him often showcases the attributes we prize most. We might think of him as a loving, grandfatherly figure; a beneficent creator; or a powerful warrior. We could think of him as a judge, never failing to be fair or just. Those who do not like him very much see him as a cosmic tyrant. So which description, if any, is correct? God, like beauty, sometimes depends upon the eye of the beholder.

An evangelist once told a story about teaching a lesson on the wrath of God. After his passionate lesson, a sweet, elderly lady approached and kindly informed him that her God was not like the one he described. Hers was not one of wrath, but of love. The God she served could never condemn sin or judge the unrighteous as guilty. As tenderly as possible, the preacher told her that his view of God was drawn straight from the pages of Scripture. Hers existed only by virtue of selective description.

It is more important now than ever to understand God as he is presented in the pages of Scripture. Human beings have a tendency to focus on what we like and dismiss or devalue what we dislike. This turns truth into a matter of personal opinion—and opinions about God always run the risk of being influenced by something other than Scripture. In the classic book *Your God is Too Small*, author J.B. Phillips explored a number of popular misconceptions about God.[1] In some cases, he may be nothing more than a guilty conscience, what Phillips called the "sleeping policeman." Some see him as a "grand old man," antiquated and outdated, useless for modern people with modern needs. He is meek-and-mild, a cosmic wimp, the ultimate pushover, the Big Guy upstairs, the eternal grandfather, or a cosmic Santa Claus. We could add a hundred other misconceptions to the list. By picking and choosing the attributes we value most, any of us can engineer a God to suit his or her individual tastes.

Custom-made versions of God are popular in the religious landscape of America because people often fail to use the Bible as a guide. Some may have ceased their investigations because they are happy with whatever mental fabrication they have constructed, or with whatever someone else has told them. Others may have stopped because they are afraid of finding something they do not like. Still others prefer only what they *do* like. In the end, we have failed to recognize God for who he is and prefer a God who does what we want or who meets our needs. This is nothing new.

A.W. Tozer lamented the state of the view of God in the mid-twentieth century, saying, "The heaviest obligation lying upon the Christian Church today is to purify and elevate her concept of God until it is once more worthy of Him—and of her."[2] Theologian Arthur Pink had an even more caustic indictment:

> The god of this century no more resembles the Sovereign of
> Holy Writ than does the dim flickering of a candle the glory of
> the midday sun. The god who is talked about in the average
> pulpit, spoken of in the ordinary Sunday school, mentioned in
> much of the religious literature of the day, and preached in most

---

1. J. B. Phillips, *Your God is Too Small* (New York, NY: Touchstone, 1997).

2. A. W. Tozer, *The Knowledge of the Holy* (New York, NY: Harper and Row, 1961), 12.

of the so-called Bible conferences, is a figment of human imagination, an invention of maudlin sentimentality. The heathen outside the pale of Christendom form gods of wood and stone, while millions of heathen inside Christendom manufacture a god out of their carnal minds.[3]

COMING TO KNOW HIM

The basis of our understanding of God lies in how we understand the Bible, in which he has revealed himself to his creation at various times and in different ways (Heb. 1:1). Theologians speak of this in two categories: general and special revelation. General revelation refers to the fact that all of creation serves as a witness to the existence of its Creator (cf. Rom 1:19-20). A fad for theologians in ages past was looking for special signs in nature that verified biblical truths (e.g., three leaf clovers serving as a symbol of the Trinity). While nature can teach us that God exists, it does not reveal many specifics about him. That is why we must turn to the second kind of revelation, which consists of anything from the supernatural realm. In biblical times, this often took the form of the prophetic word proclaimed by God's spokesmen. For those living in the 21st century, it is the written Word of God.

Our task is to see God through the eyes of the biblical authors, writers whom he inspired (2 Pet. 1:21). It only makes sense that, to understand God best, we should consult his autobiography. This in itself is a unique phenomenon in the ancient world—an anomaly in the ancient world at a time when pagan gods were not believed to either inspire sacred literature or care much about their human worshippers.

The ancients had a variety of myths and legends, but virtually nothing by way of direct revelation from the gods in written form. They believed their gods could speak to individuals in dreams and natural phenomena, but had almost no interest

---

3. Arthur Pink, *Gleanings in the Godhead* (Chicago, IL: Moody Press, 1975), 28-29.

in personal interaction with humans. Few believed their gods cared enough about mankind to reveal much about themselves. In the ancient myths, the gods wanted people to supply food and worship, but little else mattered. As long as humans performed their religious duties, the gods had no reason to intervene. Generally, it was better—and less calamitous—when the gods left people alone. This stands in stark contrast to the Bible. God expects his people to read his Word, come to know him, and to be involved with him in a personal way.

SETTING THE STAGE

Why should we study the nature and attributes of God? It is vitally important to know the nature and character of the God we serve. As Christians, our knowledge of God only increases our appreciation for him; we do not want to cheat ourselves of the enjoyment of knowing, loving, and worshipping God properly. At the same time, we do not want to be guilty of fashioning the kind of mental idol described by Pink.

We can think of our enterprise in terms of operating an automobile. Knowing how to drive a car is much different than knowing how to change a tire—except that both require some knowledge about an automobile. But knowing how to drive does not help much if we have a flat tire. If we do not know how to change a tire, we will not be able to go anywhere. Likewise, should we run out of gas, knowing how to change the oil will not help us if we do not know how to put fuel in the tank. To effectively operate an automobile, everything must be considered.

God's attributes are often classified in two categories: incommunicable and communicable. Incommunicable attributes are those that he alone possesses. Man has no functional equivalent of such attributes as omnipresence (existing in all places at the same time), aseity (self-existence), and self-sufficiency (needing nothing for existence). Communicable attributes are those that both God and man share. Love, truth, mercy, and justice are a few examples of the qualities possessed by both in some capacity or another, although God will naturally possess them in greater abundance and in purer quality than human beings.

Six blind men are brought in to describe an elephant in an Indian story made famous by poet John Godfrey Saxe. The first man feels the elephant's side, concluding that it must be something like a wall. The second feels one of the creature's tusks, and states that it is like a spear. The third grasps the elephant's truck, leading him to think that it must be like a snake. The fourth touches the elephant's leg, so he says that it is like a tree. The fifth touches an ear, and claims it is like a fan. The sixth and final wise man takes hold of the elephant's tail, stating that the elephant must be like a rope. Although each was partly in the right, all were wrong. Each man only knew of a part of the elephant, but did not have knowledge of the whole being. In attempting to reach an understanding of God, we must not be like these wise men who thought the elephant could be described by the understanding of just one part.

To truly know God, we need to realize that each one of God's attributes must be considered as part of the whole. If we believe that he is only a God of wrath, we cannot draw close to him for fear of punishment, and

> **To truly know God, we need to realize that each one of God's attributes must be considered as part of the whole.**

we will remain afraid of him. However, if we see him as only a God of love, then we have no fear of punishment. We may live our lives doing whatever we want while believing God will do nothing more than shrug his shoulders, wishing we would be more obedient but completely unable to do anything to compel us to do better. A God who is only omniscient is little more than a huge brain, good for nothing but knowing every possible fact and outcome of every event in human history—cerebral, but no more personal and loving than a laptop computer. We can see that emphasizing only one attribute of God diminishes the importance of the others. A

God who is sentimental, cruelly vindictive, weak and powerless, emotionally-driven, or all-knowing but unresponsive cannot be worshipped.

How we think about God influences what we think about him. There is a sense in which we must break up our understanding of God in basic building blocks so that we can gain a better understanding of him, but we must avoid emphasizing some of his attributes more than others. For instance, if we assume that the God of the New Testament is primarily concerned with love, then we downplay such things as wrath and justice. Likewise, if we believe that we are all just sinners in the hands of a wrathful God, then we will give little consideration to God's patience and mercy. The difficulty we face in this piecemeal approach is making sure to devote an equal amount of time to all of God's attributes.

THAT'S HEAVY

Weight was important in the Old Testament times. Abraham is described as "heavy" (*kabed*), but it had nothing to do with how much he weighed. Rather, it indicated that he was a wealthy man (Gen. 13:2). We use a similar idea of weight in common language quite frequently. If something is important, we say that it is "pressing." When we are relieved, we "feel as if a weight has been lifted" off of our shoulders. Someone "weighs in" when he gives his opinion. If he does it often enough or tries to use his influence to change the opinions of others, we say he is "throwing his weight around."

In the ancient world, the term *kabed* described a person worthy of recognition and respect.[4] The term is often used of God, who is heavy, not in a literal sense, but a spiritual one. He deserves glory and honor. Our problem is that we have consistently put God on a very strict doctrinal diet. For many, he is theologically anorexic. He is given less respect, less honor, and less glory until he is a gaunt

---

4.   John N. Oswalt, "כָּבֵד" in *Theological Wordbook of the Old Testament*, R. L. Harris, G. L. Archer Jr., & B. K. Waltke, eds. (Chicago, IL: Moody Press, 1980), 426.

shadow of the magisterial cosmic King painted by the biblical authors. David Wells describes this very phenomenon in his book, *God in the Wasteland*:

> It is one of the defining marks of Our Time that God is now weightless. I do not mean by this that he is ethereal but rather that he has become unimportant. He rests upon the world so inconsequentially as not to be noticeable. He has lost his saliency for human life. Those who assure the pollsters of their belief in God's existence may nonetheless consider him less interesting than television, his commands less authoritative than their appetites for affluence and influence, his judgment no more awe-inspiring than the evening news, and his truth less compelling than the advertisers' sweet fog of flattery and lies. That is weightlessness.[5]

Our task is to make God heavy again by understanding who he is: the one about whom the psalmists sung for joy and the one whose footsteps evil dreads. Now we begin the journey of studying the character of the one who created the universe and everything in it.

QUESTIONS TO CONSIDER

1. In your own words, who is God?

2. When you picture God in your mind, what does he look like?

3. What are some common misunderstandings about God?

4. In what ways do we think of God as "too human"?

5. How do we come to know God?

6. How should knowing God change you?

---

5. David F. Wells, *God in the Wasteland: The Reality of Truth in a World of Fading Dreams* (Grand Rapids, MI: Eerdmans, 1994), 88.

7. Which one of God's attributes do you tend to value most and why?

8. Does God care what we think of him?

CHAPTER ONE

INCOMPREHENSIBLE

K nowing God is not an easy task. It takes time, patience, and an open heart and mind. We could spend our entire lives reading the Bible and meditating on the information he has given us about himself without ever getting close to understanding him completely.

Getting to know other people can be difficult enough. We can learn a great deal about others through personal interaction. Most all of us have private information that we are reluctant or unwilling to share, but we can come to know quite a bit about others by spending time with them. By observing their behavior and mannerisms, we can pick up on their likes and dislikes and understand their preferences and nature. Even pleasant conversation can reveal volumes about a person. Then again, we might spend years with another person, and one day he or she does something that contradicts everything we thought we knew. We then think to ourselves that we never knew them at all.

It goes without saying that God is much more complex than a human being. The impossibility of having a two-way conversation with him presents unconquerable challenges. Furthermore, if God is infinite and we are finite, how would we be able to comprehend him? If we cannot know him fully, what can we know? At first glance, understanding the immensity of God seems like an ant trying to understand quantum physics.

Although substantial differences between God and humans exist, we share many similarities. If God were totally dissimilar from his creation, or "wholly other" as the German theologian Rudolf Otto once put it,[1] we could know absolutely nothing about him. He would defy our understanding from the very beginning. Thankfully, we have two aids to help us in our quest. He created us in his image, and in that likeness we find common ground between the human and the divine. Second, God speaks to us in language that we understand. He does not offer puzzles and riddles for us to solve.

CHASING A MYSTERY

Why study the incomprehensibility of God? It would seem our study is really just an exercise in self-defeat. Why bother trying to know a God who cannot be known? R. C. Sproul says,

> When teaching theology proper, I always start with God's incomprehensibility, because humility demands that we understand at the outset that we are like infants struggling to understand a genius who is speaking to us in our own terms. To whatever degree it is possible for his creatures to apprehend him, God has made himself known.[2]

We must understand that describing God as incomprehensible is not the same as claiming he is unintelligible—the two are quite different. If God is incom-

---

1. See Rudolph Otto, *The Idea of the Holy*, 2nd ed. John W. Harvey trans. (Oxford: Oxford University Press, 1958), 25-30.

2. R.C. Sproul, *Truths We Confess: A Layman's Guide to the Westminster Confession of Faith, Vol. 1: The Triune God* (Phillipsburg, NJ: Presbyterian & Reformed, 2006), 41.

prehensible, we cannot understand him exhaustively. If he were unintelligible, we could not understand him at all.

God has communicated with mankind in a way that presupposes our ability to comprehend the message. God can be known, but he resists our attempts to reduce him to more manageable proportions (this does not stop some from trying, of course).[3] If he did not, he would be finite—and would not be a God worth serving. We have limitations in our understanding of God due to the nature of our existence. Still, our understanding can still be true even if it is limited to the essential facts—basically, an approximation. We will examine three ways in which our knowledge of God is restricted.

We are limited by our minds. Unlike God, we are bound by physical limitations. If we are in one place, we cannot be somewhere else at the same time. We must travel from one place to another. We are also bound by linear time. While God sees all of human history at a single glance (cf. Isa. 46:9-10), human beings experience a progression in time. What has happened prior to the present moment is in our past and cannot be revisited. The past can be acknowledged and the present experienced, but the future remains unknown until it becomes the present. This goes far beyond our perception. We could explore just one attribute of God for a lifetime and still fail to conclude our study. Others could continue our work after our passing and not even they would be able to exhaust that one attribute.

We are limited by our own selfishness. Not only do we have a problem with our mental capacity, but a problem with our moral capacity as well. It seems that by nature human beings often value self first and foremost—something that is becoming more rampant in our culture today. The truth calls for a denial of our own selfish wants and pleasures. Some people prefer error to the truth (John 3:19-21), and self and Satan can prevent us from seeing it (Rom. 1:28; 2 Cor. 4:4). Too often people abandon the truth in order to do and believe as they please, twisting

---

3. This is usually done by making God more like us. It has been said in the beginning, God made man in his image, and mankind has been trying to return the favor ever since.

the biblical portrait of God to suit their own tastes.

We are limited by the revelation we have received. The apostle Paul warned others "not to go beyond what is written" (1 Cor. 4:6). Human beings are not free to go beyond what Scripture states. Whatever is written has been recorded for our knowledge. Should we go beyond what has been revealed, we risk generating a mental idol. Instead of worshipping the one true God, we would instead worship a god who is like the God of the Bible, but with imaginative and forbidden additions.

THE GOD YOU WANT

Biblical scholar N.T. Wright tells a story about browsing in a second-hand bookshop when he discovered a book entitled, *The God I Want*. After thinking about it for a while, he said,

> The God I Want? Left to myself, the god I want is a god who will give me what I want. He – or more likely it – will be a projection of my desires. At the grosser level, this will lead me to one of the more obvious pagan gods or goddesses, who offer their devotees money, or sex, or power (as Marx, Freud and Nietzsche pointed out). All idols started out life as the god somebody wanted.[4]

We often try to picture God in some way. People are physical beings, so it only makes sense that we would try to have a mental depiction of God. But the very attempt to wrap our minds around such an image would not do him justice. He is not a man, and we are not divine. No matter how great and powerful that image is, it is still a finite portrait of an infinite being.

Some people think of God as an old man, but he is neither human nor old

---

4. N.T. Wright, *For All God's Worth: True Worship and Calling of the Church* (Grand Rapids: Eerdmans, 1997), 23.

in human terms. Others envision him as a bright light. While he does sometimes manifest his glory in a brilliant radiance, that does not capture the essence of his being. Others view him as a shepherd—a very biblical idea, but an anthropomorphic image still. Some might suggest a picture of Jesus as the human face of the Father. This is not far off the mark, but then again Jesus is not identical with the God the Father. He is co-equal, but they are not one and the same in every respect. Regardless of the image, God transcends everything we have at our disposal to understand him completely.

We often describe God by comparing him to people. The Bible speaks of God's arm, eyes, hands, and even his nose. Language has its limits, but that does not mean that our language is useless, only inadequate. What does our image say to us about how we understand God? Does that image say something to us about who we are?

Earthy, concrete images fill the Old Testament, such as God's possession of the earth or its inhabitants, whereas we are more prone to using abstract phrases such as commenting on God's self-sufficiency. The difference between these two is that the first is a figurative expression. In using the second, we are no longer speaking in concrete terms, but the two are still relatively equal, since we understand sufficiency from a human standpoint of sufficiency. These terms are both expressions of human thought.

Doctrines are ideas or concepts expressed with words. Words themselves are symbols that serve to represent something. For instance, the word "apple" is not the same thing as a real apple. One is the object; the other is the word describing the object. Language cannot capture who God is, since the very nature of God defies description. We can only understand an approximation of what ideas, concepts, and images are able to communicate.

THE BIG REVEAL

Even though we run up against the boundaries of human language, we may speak adequately and meaningfully because God is a God of revelation. Christianity is a revealed religion. Our faith and practice is rooted in the Word rather than in our own imaginations. Though the secret things belong to God, what he has revealed belongs to us. It is for our understanding and usage. We can understand enough to rejoice, adore, and serve him while looking forward to spending eternity with him.

God has volunteered an incredible amount of personal information about himself. In a sense, the Bible is his autobiography. But God cannot tell us everything—no number of library shelves could contain that much information. Despite the complexity of the brain, the human cranium simply cannot contain that much data. It would be like trying to fit a universe into a thimble.

We are not the first ones to struggle with the incomprehensibility of God. Apart from bringing up discussions of the problems of suffering and evil, Job deals with the difficulty of knowing the Almighty. Job did not understand the reasons for his suffering, but that is not the most amazing part of the story. In Job 38:1-40:2, God appears to Job in a whirlwind and asks the patriarch a series of questions that reveal the boundaries of his knowledge. Job has already said, "Who does great things beyond searching out, and marvelous things beyond number. Behold, he passes by me, and I see him not; he moves on, but I do not perceive him. Behold, he snatches away; who can turn him back? Who will say to him, 'What are you doing?'" (Job 9:10-12).

When appearing to Job, God says, ""Who is this that darkens counsel by words without knowledge? Dress for action like a man; I will question you, and you make it known to me. "Where were you when I laid the foundation of the earth? Tell me, if you have understanding. Who determined its measurements—surely you know! Or who stretched the line upon it?" (Job 38:2-5). Job cannot answer any of God's questions. Neither can we.

Man cannot see God, number his works, or restrain his movements. God will do exactly as he pleases without any input from his creation. Paul echoes Job's sentiments when he writes, "For the word of the cross is folly to those who are perishing, but to us who are being saved it is the power of God. For it is written, 'I will destroy the wisdom of the wise, and the discernment of the discerning I will thwart.' Where is the one who is wise? Where is the scribe? Where is the debater of this age? Has not God made foolish the wisdom of the world?" (1 Cor. 1:18-21).

In the divine interrogation, the result is that Job and his friends are put in their places. They cannot answer the questions, and we cannot answer many more today than they could then because human reason is insufficient. Job bows before the glory of God and declares that the things the Lord has told him surpass his understanding. The New Testament counterpart to this confession of limitation is Paul's exclamation, "Oh, the depth of the riches and wisdom and knowledge of God! How unsearchable are his judgments and how inscrutable his ways! "For who has known the mind of the Lord, or who has been his counselor?" (Rom. 11:33-34).

Other passages speak of the surpassing greatness of God. Paul tells the Ephesians that the love of Christ "surpasses knowledge" (Eph. 3:19). The apostle also tells the Philippians "the peace of God ... surpasses all understanding" (Phil. 4:7). Other things that defy our understanding are God's greatness (Psa. 145:3), understanding (Psa. 147:5), knowledge (Psa. 139:6), and his riches, wisdom, judgments, and ways (Rom. 11:33). Can human beings know about these things? Absolutely. We just cannot know them exhaustively.

There is a benefit in being unable to fully understand God. We will never exhaust our understanding of him. No matter how much we study and learn, we cannot ever sit back on our laurels and assume there is no more work to do. The pursuit of godly knowledge should be a delight to us. If it can never be known in its entirety, then we will always have a source of enjoyment as we search the unfathomable riches of God as he is revealed in his Word. There is no danger of us ever getting bored with him.

Once we experience something, we often grow tired of it. As the old saying goes, "familiarity breeds contempt." We get tired of repetition and of routine, and people today are often spiritually bored and have developed a "been there, done that" attitude. We pick out classes at church based on, in part, whether we've heard the material before. Sermons that cover familiar topics are often quickly tuned out. Too accustomed to the media's rapid-fire presentation of images, sounds, and information, we have little time for extended or carefully-developed treatments of subjects.

Children never seem to tire of what is familiar. The same books, songs, pictures, and stories seem to captivate them over and over again. However, as we get older, we quickly tire of such things. But what about a subject we can never master, a subject that forever eludes our complete understanding? That is God.

Scientists are forever interested in their respective fields of study because mankind constantly learns new things. We make new discoveries, push past old boundaries, and invent new technologies to make the world smaller, more comprehensible, more accessible. And yet the objects of scientific examination are necessarily finite. As things existing in time and space, these subjects of human inquiry could be exhausted. And yet we, as Christians, seem to bore easily of spiritual matters.

> The incomprehensibility of God should push us to ever-increasing intensity of investigation.

Strangely enough, we tend to tire quickly of the one limitless, boundless, infinite Being in the universe. The incomprehensibility of God should push us to ever-increasing intensity of investigation, and the unfathomable nature of his being should invite our curiosity. His indescribable holiness can cause us to weep rivers of tears, but the boundless limits of his love transforms that mourning into celebration. If we become bored of God, we can be bored of anything.

NICE TO MEET YOU

While God is ultimately incomprehensible, he also wants his creation to know him (cf. John 10:27). When we think of something as incomprehensible, we usually think of it being completely unknowable. However, this is not the case with God. He reveals himself in ways that can be grasped by the human mind. For instance, Psalm 19:1-2 says: "The heavens declare the glory of God, and the sky above proclaims his handiwork. Day to day pours out speech, and night to night reveals knowledge."

Paul echoes this sentiment to Christians in Rome when he says, "For what can be known about God is plain to them, because God has shown it to them. For his invisible attributes, namely, his eternal power and divine nature, have been clearly perceived, ever since the creation of the world, in the things that have been made. So they are without excuse" (Rom. 1:19-20).

The way a person approaches the study of God tells everything about his idea of God. Is he the God of the Bible or just another deity of human invention? The attributes of the deity involved will make the difference whether one holds to truth or opinion. Does the Lord reveal himself to man, or is it our duty to discover him through our own mental wrestling match? Is he unchanging, or do his characteristics change based on the perspective of each particular theologian? Is his nature absolute, or is it relative to the individual? The ultimate conclusion to this pursuit is the difference between truth and myth. Either God is true and deserves to be worshipped with every fiber of our being, or he is the world's greatest lie, and we should be ashamed to worship him. So we begin our exploration of God's nature and attributes, knowing that we cannot know him fully, yet left in a state of wonder and even excitement at this God whose greatness defies our attempts to put him in a convenient little box.

Having a relationship with God is predicated on our ability to know him. The inability of people to understand the divine was a common feature of pagan religion. People tried to placate the deities they served, but otherwise hoped that their gods did not notice them. The revelation of God was much different. The very fact that he reveals himself to man indicates that he wants to be known. In the world of that time, the inspired biblical authors revealed a bright, shining light of truth to a world living in darkness.

QUESTIONS TO CONSIDER

1. What does it mean to know God?

2. What has God done to ensure we can know him?

3. What are some differences between getting to know God and another person?

4. What is the most incomprehensible aspect about God?

5. What is the difference between God being incomprehensible and being unintelligible?

6. Does the phrase, "What you don't know can't hurt you" apply to God? In what way?

7. In what ways can God be too familiar?

8. What is the difference between knowing God and knowing about God?

CHAPTER TWO

INFINITY & ASEITY

W hen we consider something that is infinite in scope, it is a new dimension or category of thought both mysterious and troublesome. One way we speak of God most often is by negation. That is, we say what he is not. For instance, God is not sinful, finite, changeable, or fallible. He is different from us in many ways. God is not only unlimited, he is illimitable. Even those things formerly though of as inexhaustible or limitless (such as the universe itself) seem to have limits. God does not.

There are two categories of God's infinity. The first of these is infinity in respect to time. Time simply does not apply to an eternal being. He has no beginning or end, seeing all time equally. The second category is space. He is unlimited in his being in that he does not have spatial dimensions, being present everywhere at once (called "omnipresence"). We might say that in these things God is immeasurable.

Human beings measure a lot of things. Our thoughts and actions are governed by limitations that we take care not to exceed. We have to see how much money we have before we can buy something. We consider how much time a task will take, and we may be hesitant to start something if there is not enough time to finish it.

As finite creatures, we have to break things down into pieces so we can understand them. Usually, something that is "immeasurable" carries with it the understanding that we will not be able to mentally grasp whatever it is that we are studying.

If asked, "How do you picture God?" anyone could think of dozens of different images. Some see God as being obscured by a brilliant radiance surrounding him. Others may picture him as the King on his heavenly throne (certainly a biblical idea). In Michelangelo's Sistine Chapel, the Renaissance painter depicted him as a powerful, muscled figure with white hair and a flowing beard. In human perception, God does indeed seem to be old, but we show the limitations of our own minds when we envision him as an elderly man.

God is the master of time. He knows everything that will happen, including the exact point of the end of human history. This is not to say that God will re-write history.[1] Everything that has happened has fulfilled some part of the divine plan for humankind. While we might want to go back and erase such events as wars and plagues, they have played important roles in human history. We may not understand why such things took place, but we may be confident that they have served some greater purpose in the plans of God (cf. Rom. 8:28). God's timelessness is a difficult concept to grasp.

We have no personal experience of an eternal existence. Instead, we gauge the passing of time in various ways, ranging from watches to calendars. Regardless of the instrument used, we measure by the distance between the motions of two or more things or events. The only way we are aware of time is by motion or activity. If there were no objects to create motion, could we truly measure time? For us, this would be a difficult—if not impossible—task.

Time is a precious commodity for those whom it binds. We are always con-

---

1.   Some would contend that God is unable to re-write history, since the combination of his foreknowledge and his perfection would have required him, by nature, to work in the best possible way from the beginning. To say that God would need to redo the past would be for God to admit that he made a mistake that needed to be corrected.

scious of the time because we only have a limited amount. We are consumed with deadlines, ETAs, and the like. Life is furiously hectic when we try to cram too many things into the limited space that we have. If we do not do enough, we feel as if we have wasted our time. Time charts the spaces from one activity to the next. We only have so much of it, and then our time is over. If we look on a tombstone, we see two dates that succinctly sum up the whole of life—one for our entrance into this world and the other for our exit.

> **There was never a time when God was not. There never will be a time when God will not be. There is only the eternal with God.**

We are accustomed to speaking of persons in qualified terms with respect to time when we look at history. We talk about people using the present, past, and future tenses. But God is always spoken of in the present tense. There was never a time when God was not. There never will be a time when God will not be. There is only the eternal with God. We can speak of his reactions in the past or future tenses, but with regard to his person and being, there is no past or future, only an unchanging is.

NO THING LIKE NOTHING

It is interesting to think about the fact that there is really no such thing as nothing.[2] If it were said that nothing were "no thing," then it is the absence of something, which means that nothing is indeed something. If nothing were actual-

---

2.   There is a very real sense in which "nothing" cannot exist, for there is no place where God is not. Even in the Old Testament, Solomon hinted at this fact when he said "But will God indeed dwell on the earth? Behold, heaven and the highest heaven cannot contain you; how much less this house that I have built!" (1 Kings 8:27).

ly no thing, then it would not exist, nor would we be able to talk about it. This may seem like a pointless mental exercise in abstract thought, but it certainly applies to the study of God. It applies precisely because there is never any place in this universe where there is nothing because there is no place where God is not present.

To be infinite is to be unlimited. There is no end to God's being or perfection; he has no boundaries as we do. If we are sitting in a chair, we can look to the other side of the room and see space that is beyond us. God cannot see something from a distance, nor does he need to get closer to something in order to see it more clearly.[3] He's everywhere at all times, and his being fills all of reality. Outer space may have places that are devoid of any matter, but it is not completely empty, since God is present. Just because there is no physical matter does not mean that nothing's there. He is not bound by physicality as human beings are, but this does not mean he's spread out across the universe with different parts located in different places. He's everywhere at once.

God fills everything, but that does not mean God is everything. There is a great distinction between God and his creation, and the two are not to be confused. Pantheism says that nature exists within God. While it is true that we owe him our existence, we are not an extension of him. We are different, being finite, physical, and localized to a single place at any given time. Our being is derived from God. We do not possess the power of being on our own.

Jeremiah complains about the false teachings of his prophetic peers (Jer. 23). Their messages do irreparable harm to the people. But Yahweh is already aware of what these evil men are doing. He says, "'Am I a God at hand, declares the LORD, and not a God far away? Can a man hide himself in secret places so that I cannot see him? declares the LORD. Do I not fill heaven and earth? declares

---

3.   Perhaps the lone exception here is in Genesis 11:7 when God gets a closer look at the Tower of Babel and confuses the language of those gathered there. What Moses is attempting to convey here, however, is the smallness of humanity's efforts in light of their goal to build a tower that reaches up to the heavens. In one sense, this could be interpreted as almost comedic.

the LORD" (Jer. 23:23-24). This statement indirectly refers to the omnipresence of God.[4] Since there is no place where God does not exist, he tells his prophet that he has indeed seen the terrible things done by false prophets. They have spoken words the Lord never gave, and they announce dreams that Yahweh did not send. The Lord does not need his prophet to inform him because he already knows.

God is not only everywhere but is everywhere in the fullness of his being. Although he is present everywhere, we should not think of him as having one part here, another part there. This is called the *simplicity* of God. This does not mean that he is easy to understand, but rather that he is not a composite being made up of different parts. He is everywhere with the totality of his being. He has no center or extremities.

The study of God is very complicated. It is always difficult to study something so different from what we experience. God is not made up of a combination of parts. He is not complex in the sense that he is divided up into different attributes, such as love, mercy, holiness, etc. We cannot break him down into bits and pieces. He loves with a love that is holy, judges with absolute justice, and is powerful with infinite power.

These concepts are exceedingly difficult to explore. There is always the risk of running into distortion during the pursuit of simplicity. What does it mean for God to be everywhere in all his perfection, literally at our fingertips? We may think of him as "wholly other," but he is not far removed from us. We have to understand that the barrier that separates us is dimensional, not geographical.

We have the ability to pray to God anytime, anywhere because of his omnipresence. The pagan gods did not have such ability. We see this in the divine showdown between Elijah and the four hundred priests of Ba'al. The prophet suggests that his opponents "cry aloud, for [Ba'al] is a god. Either he is musing, or he is relieving himself, or he is on a journey, or perhaps he is asleep and must be awakened" (1 Kings 18:27). Ba'al was not omnipresent.

---

4. This is also called *ubiquity* (from the Latin for "equal whereness").

The prophets of Ba'al were very poor theologians. Elijah, an astute man of God, knew the limitations of the pagan gods and taunted the false prophets, essentially asking them, "Is Ba'al asleep, or on a journey, or in the bathroom perhaps?" The pagan mindset could not conceive of their gods in anything but human terms. They ate, drank, enjoyed physical relationships, and could die.

While Christians often think of God in human terms, we understand that to do so does not do justice to the marvelous infinity of God. There is no beginning or end to God, since he has no limitations. Time and space have no effect upon him like they do us. This is what theologians mean in using the term *immensity*. While this often refers to the physical size of something, in theology it refers to God who is everywhere at all times. The only difference is that he is always present everywhere with the fullness of his being. All that he is, is everywhere at the same time.

WHO CREATED GOD?

The quality that sets God apart from everything else is his aseity (from the Latin *a se*, meaning "from himself").[5] Scripture affirms that God does not need any part of creation. This applies not only to his existence, but to everything else as well. The apostle Paul tells us this when he says, "The God who made the world and everything in it, being Lord of heaven and earth, does not live in temples made by man, nor is he served by human hands, as though he needed anything, since he himself gives to all mankind life and breath and everything" (Acts 17:24-25). God does not need anything in creation.

It is not unusual for an unknowing person to assume God created mankind because he was lonely or because he needed something or someone to govern. If this were true, then God would not be completely independent of his creation. He would not be complete in himself and would, therefore, be imperfect. A number of texts militate against this idea.

---

5.   This attribute is also called *self-existence* or *independence*.

Jesus notes that he shared glory with the Father before the world was made (John 17:5). Only a few verses later, Jesus says that he and the Father shared love and communication before the foundation of the world (John 17:15). Clearly, the members of the Trinity enjoyed a kind of fellowship that did not include a necessity for mankind. The three Persons were entirely complete and self-sufficient before the world was created.

The difference between God and his creation is incredible. The creation owes its existence to a higher power, while God owes his existence to no one—not even himself (he is self-existent, not self-creating). We are finite creatures that have a beginning point, while God is eternal. He is immense in his deity, while we are quite puny in comparison. Our God exists in a fundamentally different way than we do.

There is a description of God's aseity that begins with one of his names (actually, it is perhaps his most important name used in Scripture). We must first recognize that God has revealed himself to us by way of different names. He is personal. There is a history of a relationship between him and his people as recorded in Scripture. When we pray, we do not refer to God in some abstract sense as "Supreme Being," "Higher Power," or "Absolute Person."

God has a personal name—several, in fact, but none more important than the one revealed in Exodus 3. In the familiar story, Moses happens upon a bush that is engulfed in flames yet is not consumed by them. God commands him to take off his sandals because Moses is standing on holy ground. Here the Lord reveals himself by saying, "I am the God of…Abraham, the God of Isaac, and the God of Jacob" (Exod. 3:6). He then tells Moses that he must go to Pharaoh. Though Moses questions his own ability, God gives him the promise of his presence. It is here that God refers to himself as Yahweh.

Yahweh is God's personal, covenant name. There seem to be several ideas this name communicates. First, God is a person, a being. And since God simply is, he exists without support from anything else. Human beings rely on things like food and air to sustain us, and we have only a limited amount of time to live. God has neither. The past, present, and future are three distinct modes of time for us because we are temporal creatures. God is not bound by time.

One point that provoked incredible hostility during Christ's ministry was his use of the phrase "I am" (Greek *ego eimi*). This is what the translators of the Septuagint used when they translated the phrase "I AM."[6] Jesus makes a connection between God and himself. One of the most prominent uses of this is when he says, "Before Abraham was, I am" (John 8:58). Jesus uses for himself the same designation that reveals God's eternal character.

In looking at the story of Moses, some believe that God is not really giving a name at all, as if he meant to say, "I am who I am, and never you mind—just do what I tell you!" Instead, Moses serves as a spokesman for God, much like a diplomat to the Egyptian court. It would only be natural for God to tell Moses in whose name the fledgling prophet would be sent.

Yahweh is the sacred name of God that no Jew would dare pronounce. It serves as a testimony to God's aseity. He has the power of being, who exists in an eternal state of is and self-existence with no need of help or support. The existence of everything else in reality is derived from, and dependent upon, him. The Lord does not experience a birthday, an anniversary, or retirement.

Nothing has the power of spontaneous generation. That is, nothing cannot suddenly become something. Matter cannot magically appear. Something had to exist in order for the universe to exist. Atheists will claim that at the very beginning, the entire universe was condensed into a tiny ball of matter the size of a proton. Then the Big Bang happened, and the universe appeared. But this theory does not explain where matter came from. We know that matter cannot be eternal, so what's the only other explanation? There must be something else that has eternal existence. The only other explanation is God. If there ever was a time when there

---

6.   The Septuagint is the Greek translation of the Old Testament, dating to approximately 250-200 B.C. It is often abbreviated LXX (Roman numerals for seventy, which refers to the approximate number of translators).

was absolutely nothing, then there would be nothing now. Something has to have eternal being before anything else can be.

Where did God come from? He could not have made himself. In order to create himself, he would have to already exist before he brought himself into existence. Logically, nothing can create itself, not even God. We must simply admit that God is eternal and everything else exists because of him.

QUESTIONS TO CONSIDER

1. What does it mean for God to be infinite?

2. How does idolatry do injustice to God?

3. How easy is it for people to make mental idols of God? Why?

4. What does it mean for God to be self-existent?

5. Does God's self-existence mean he created himself? Why not?

6. In what ways does God's existence differ from ours?

CHAPTER THREE

OMNIPRESENCE

When I was in college, I could not decide what I wanted to do with my life. It was my senior year and graduation was swiftly approaching. Every week, some of my friends gathered to watch wrestling. Then it hit me: I would present God with a couple of choices and let him decide! I would either go to Atlanta, Georgia and train to become a professional wrestler, or pursue a graduate degree in Bible. I told everyone about my plan, and most people thought I was joking. I got information on both options, sent my application off for school, and waited. I was accepted into seminary a couple of months later. It was probably for the best. The prospect of running around in public wearing a form-fitting spandex costume is not quite as exciting now after some time for reflection.

Wrestling was a popular sport in the ancient world, and it makes an appearance of sorts in the Old Testament. In Genesis 32:22-31, Jacob spends the night alone by the Jabbok River. A mysterious man approaches him. The two wrestle all night long, and when dawn is beginning to break, the man tells Jacob to let loose of him. Jacob agrees to do so only if he can get a blessing, which the man provides. Jacob soon realizes the man was no ordinary person. He has been in the presence of Yahweh. He names the place Penuel, which means "the face of God."

Jacob had a profound sense of the presence of God. It is something that evokes a sense of fear and even dread when he realizes it. But God's presence is quite unlike that of any other being. At times he appears in specific places, as in his wrestling match with Jacob. But he is also spirit, and he is everywhere. We are surrounded by him every moment of our lives, yet like Jacob we often have little awareness of it.

HE WALKS EVERYWHERE INCOGNITO

The omnipresence of God is one of three "omni" attributes, along with omnipotence and omniscience. It means that God is present everywhere, at all times, with all the fullness of his being. God is in all places at all times. This is described by various theological terms, such as ubiquity or immensity. Whatever term we use, it is quite impossible for finite beings to understand God's infinite presence. Even the term infinity is a mathematical idea that reduces something uncountable or unquantifiable to a concept that can be grasped by the human mind.

Central to the belief in God's omnipresence is the fact that he is spirit. Obviously, he could not have a physical body and still be omnipresent, or there would be room for nothing else in all creation. God is real, but invisible, and has a particular uniqueness in that he exists without a physical form. God may not occupy physical space, but his existence covers every inch of reality.

When we say that God is a spirit, we are not saying that he is some kind of disembodied ghost or phantom. It simply means that he is not a material being (Luke 24:39). Because he is a spirit, he can be present everywhere. When we ask for information about a person (on an application, perhaps), right after his name we ask for where he lives, and phone numbers for her home and workplace. In other words, we want to know where we can find him or her. Unlike God, we can only be one place at a time.

Some use a sense of direction when talking about God's location, as if he is limited in some way. He is somewhere "up" in heaven or "inside" our hearts. However, we cannot actually point him out in one direction, since he is not located in a singular place because he is everywhere at once. The fact that he is a spirit is part of what makes him able to be everywhere at once, existing in all places without being physically confined to a single location.

Human beings are different from God in that we cannot live on earth as we know it without physical bodies. We often equate a person's body with that person. Just because we cannot see a person's soul does not mean that that person is not real. Likewise, just because we cannot see God does not mean that he does not exist (cf. 1 Tim. 1:17). Just because God is invisible does not mean that he is any less real.

One of the basic descriptions of God in the New Testament is found in the Gospel of John. In the fourth chapter, Jesus rests beside the well at Sychar in Samaria. At about the sixth hour a Samaritan woman comes to the well to draw her water. Jesus, tired and thirsty, asks her for a drink. This should not be surprising, since Jesus took human form in his mission on earth. It is true that God is spirit, but Jesus was both fully God and fully man, with all the physical limitations and needs that a human being possesses (cf. Heb. 2:17; 4:15).

This episode is a strange one indeed. A morally perfect Jewish rabbi speaking with a sinful Samaritan woman would have violated every cultural norm of the first century. To say that Samaritans and Jews had no dealings with each other was an understatement (John 4:9). These two groups hated each other passionately. History records incidents of violence in the centuries prior to Christ's birth. Yet it is in an episode with this nameless social outcast that Jesus reveals something incredibly important about his Father.

The Samaritan woman questioned Jesus concerning the proper place to worship God. In a sense, Jesus gently draws her into a theological discussion. The Samaritans believed that Mount Gerazim was the only place to worship him. Though there were thirteen different mountains mentioned in the Pentateuch, they believed that these were thirteen different names for Gerazim.

Christ says that there would come a day when it would not matter where believers worshipped God. With the arrival of the Messiah, there would be no argument whether Gerazim or Jerusalem was the appropriate place. He would make the Temple obsolete. God would no longer be concerned with the "where," but the "who" and "how."

Jesus makes a vitally important statement when he says, "God is spirit" (John 4:24). It is essential to note that he does not say that God is "a spirit." This would imply that there are other spirits besides him. This small distinction would do irreparable damage to the doctrine of God. It would demote him to a lesser status as merely one spirit among many.

It is quite remarkable to think of the universality of God. While lecturing in New Zealand in 2008, a group of us went to visit some local astronomers one night. They gave us a glimpse of the night sky though some extremely powerful telescopes. As I peered in the lens, I saw an unmistakable shape: the planet Saturn. It did not look anything like the pictures with beautiful colors in a copy of National Geographic or an astronomy magazine. I saw only a tiny silver image in the eyepiece, but I could make out its unmistakable rings. I had been in love with astronomy as a little boy, and seeing a planet millions of miles away was thrilling, and, naturally, got my imagination going. I thought back to old episodes of *Star Trek* and *Star Wars* and a dozen other science fiction tales of distant galaxies and extraterrestrial life. Then I thought, "God knows what the weather conditions on Saturn are right now." In the farthest reaches of the universe, God knows the most intimate details of each star, each planet, and every single atom in existence. He knows the positions and movements of everything from a galaxy to an electron. And he not only knows it through observation, but he has personal knowledge of each square micrometer of the universe because he is present everywhere, at all times, with the fullness of his being.

A GOD UNLIKE ALL OTHERS

Early church fathers claimed that God had no "passions," but this does not mean God is devoid of any emotions. Scripture clearly indicates that he loves his people, hates sin, and feels both joy and disappointment. The term "passion" is a reference to bodily passions or desires. He does not have a stomach, so he has no desire for food. He has no reproductive system, so he has no desire for sexual intimacy. This is a major difference between Yahweh and the ancient gods, who did hunger for food, drink, and sexual relations with other gods and with humans.

We should be wary of thinking that God is an impersonal force when we speak of his being a spirit (John 4:24). He is a being that lacks physical form, but he is also very real. He is not a feeling, idea, or some nebulous force that permeates the universe. He is a God who is immaterial but also one who is very personal. The inability to detect God with our five senses is troubling for some—especially in an age dominated by science—since we use our senses to stay in contact with the world. With an invisible God runs the risk of being out of sight, out of mind, and sadly, many times he is exactly that, even for Christians.

On the other hand, making God visible reduces him to something conceivable, something that can be quantified and understood by the human mind. That is why graven images of God were banned under the Mosaic Law (Exod. 20:4). To depict God was to limit him, and to do so would give the worshiper the impression that he could control him—a common feature of ancient paganism.

Some unbelievers say, "Show me God, and I'll be a Christian" or "If God would reveal himself to me right here, I would be a believer in no time flat." Actually, they would not. They would find a way to dismiss him, like Ebenezer Scrooge who explained away the ghost of his former partner Tom Marley in Charles Dickens' *A Christmas Carol*. When the deceased Marley asks why Scrooge does not trust his senses, he explains,

[A] little thing affects them. A slight disorder of the stomach makes them cheats. You may be an undigested bit of beef, a blot of mustard, a crumb of cheese, a fragment of an underdone potato. There's more of gravy than of grave about you, whatever you are!

The modern atheist would give an answer a bit more sophisticated, perhaps attributing his experience to sleep deprivation, a daydream, a delusion, the misfire of a synapse, or an optical illusion. Still, the answer would be the same: Something has affected my senses, and that is why I cannot trust them. Since I cannot trust them, then whatever evidence I seem to perceive about the existence of God is invalid.

This unique nature of God as spirit, invisible, unmoved by physical passions or desires, can be quite comforting. There are times when every human being experiences the dark night of the soul. There is a hurt, a longing, an emptiness, a hollowness that pulls us down into darker and darker depths and saps our strength. We lose interest in virtually everything and obsess over that one thing that has drawn the curtains of darkness over us. In a time like this, how useful is an idol? A little divine statuette that cannot hear, speak, or see? Moreover, how able is it to comfort, to assure?

Understanding God's presence is comforting. He is present everywhere, in all things and through all things. The Holy Spirit intercedes for us with groanings that cannot be uttered by human lips (Rom. 8:26). It seems that sometimes life reduces us to the point of incomprehensibility. We have a hard time formulating our thoughts, and a harder time trying to express them. We do not know what we want and no amount of thought or planning will help us define it further, much less articulate it so that someone else could understand.

> **Understanding God's presence is comforting. He is present everywhere, in all things and through all things.**

There are times of suffering when only a groan can capture the true nature of our hurt. And that is exactly what the Holy Spirit does. With a language that captures the incomprehensible in a way that only the divine can understand, he intercedes for us with a guttural, visceral moan that communicates in a way that is more effective than the most brilliant philosopher or the wisest sage. It is elementary in its simplicity, yet unfathomable in its complexity.

WHERE TWO OR THREE ARE GATHERED

Some people find worship boring. They mumble through the songs, nod off during the sermon, and allow their minds to wander during prayer and communion. What if God came to church one day? Imagine that he sits down beside us and says, "I just wanted to see how things are going down here." I imagine that we would perk up and be more engaged in worship. But is he not always there beside us? We do not worship because God is watching. That would be nothing more than simple appeasement. We worship God because he deserves worship and because it is something for which man was made. And, being made for worship, man was intended to enjoy it.

God's presence is no routine event. He manifests himself at various times in Scripture in something called a theophany. A theophany is some kind of visible manifestation of God. Famous examples include the burning bush, the whirlwind in the book of Job, or the small, still voice that called out to the prophet Elijah. The human responses to the theophanies in which God appears range from joy to silence to abject terror, but we never find boredom or malaise as a reaction to God's appearance. God can be exciting, mystifying, and terrifying, but never boring.

We can see the remarkable presence of God in a story involving one of the most famous prophets of Scripture. In the eighth century BC, God called Jonah to preach to the city of Nineveh. Usually prophets preached to God's own people in the attempt to get them to see the folly of their ways and return to a state of covenant obedience. Occasionally, however, prophets preached to outsiders, and as far as outsiders went, Assyria was one of the worst. The prophet Nahum called Nineveh "the bloody city" (Nah. 3:1), and for good reason. The Assyrians, in general, terrorized the ancient world. Their policy, like others before and after them, was to make examples of those who rebelled against them. They enforced heavy taxation on the peoples they conquered, who often rebelled. Invariably, the Assyrians would go on campaign to re-subjugate these rulers, decimating their people in the process.

Depictions of soldiers pulling out victims' tongues, breaking their legs, and carrying severed heads are a frequent sight in Assyrian art. We can imagine the revulsion Jonah must have felt when God asked him to preach not only to the Assyrians, but to the Ninevites. Nineveh was not the political capital, but the religious center of Assyria. God was essentially asking him to go straight into the heart of the most violent pagan people the world had ever known. Instead, Jonah fled the scene, going down to Joppa on the Mediterranean coast to find a ship going in the opposite direction. It is here that Jonah enrolls into the school of Yahweh, getting a refresher course in the presence of God.

The Bible is quite clear about the presence of God, especially in the Old Testament. The story of Joseph makes it clear that even in Egypt, God has power, and the story of Jonah does the same. This is especially important because those in the ancient Near East thought of their gods as being limited by geography. Gods simply did not have much power outside their territory. It would have been easy for the Jews to adopt this limited way of thinking about God. After all, they seem to have adopted just about everything else in terms of religion. One of God's names was El Shaddai (a name that probably means something like "God of the Mountain"), usually translated as "God Almighty." The Arameans believed that God's power was confined to the mountainous areas of Palestine (1 Kings 20:23). Jonah seems to have thought similarly, if only for a time. He tries to flee the presence of God, but runs into something much more terrifying: the realization that God is everywhere.

The prophet boards a ship headed to Tarshish, which may have been located in Spain. As far as Jonah is concerned, it is on the other end of the earth. But during the voyage the ship runs into some rough waters courtesy of the Spirit of God. The crew tries to find out which god has been offended so that they can appease him. They quickly discover that it is Jonah's God who has sent the storm, and the prophet himself is responsible for the storm being sent. After doing their best to row back to land, the only option left is to heave Jonah overboard. Once the prophet hits the water, the storm stops, and Jonah's journey to salvation begins.

In the blackness of the briny deep, Jonah felt as if his very life was being drained (Jon. 2:7). It must have been terrifying to be pitched into the sea, especially since very few people in the ancient world outside of sailors could swim. The sensation of drowning is a terrifying one, and Jonah probably experienced it to the fullest.

The exact nature of the creature that swallowed Jonah is debated. The Hebrew text calls it a "big fish," but Hebrew is a highly flexible language, so much so that "big fish" really does not mean much more than "large aquatic creature." Whether it was a shark, whale, or anything else is unimportant. What is important is that God demonstrates that he goes where no deity has gone before.

In Psalm 139, David describes the remarkable presence of God as something from which he could not escape. For David, the infinity of God meant the absolute guarantee of his presence wherever he went, whether it was to the heights of heaven or the depths of the grave (Psa. 139:7-10). God is ever-present, which means he is always accessible. Some people fear being alone, but if God can be with us at all times and in all places, then we are never truly alone. Whether it is at the pinnacle of the heavens or the depths of the grave, God is there always.

QUESTIONS TO CONSIDER

1. Where do you think God is right now?

2. What are some of the problems with having a God who is unseen?

3. Are there any qualifications on God's presence, either here or in eternity?

4. How easy is it to fall prey to doubts in light of God's invisibility?

5. Who were some biblical characters who tried to hide or run away from God?

6. What does it mean to you personally to know, that no matter how lonely you are, you are never truly alone?

CHAPTER FOUR

OMNIPOTENCE

E verything in our experience as human beings is conditional. Sooner or later we are going to fail. No matter how hard we try, what precautions we take, or what plans we make, every one of us will come up short—and sooner rather than later. We are bound by countless limitations physically, mentally, and spiritually, and we ordinarily judge what we can or cannot do in light of those self-perceived limitations. We are so used to thinking of life in terms of these limitations that we rarely, if ever, consider what it would be like to have no limitations.

Omnipotence literally means "all power." God is the one who has the fullness of power within himself. No other being is powerful in a way that he is not, nor is any other being powerful to the same extent that the Lord is. God's might is unchallengeable. Other beings must acquire power in order to have it. The athlete lifts weights and conditions his body. The entrepreneur builds his corporate empire. The politician rises from the rank-and-file of local government. Even Popeye has to eat his spinach.

Our limitations are often the inspiration for jokes. When I was in college, I would often visit a friend who lived in his mom's three-story house. The stairway going up to his bedroom was narrow, much more so than the ones in my house. Several times I got in a hurry and managed to trip on my way up, much to the amusement of everyone else. I can still hear their peals of laughter. I simply was not used to the narrowness of the stairs. We often encounter, and even expect, other physical limitations such as this during our lifetimes.

GOD DOES NOT FALL UP THE STAIRS

God expresses his power in different ways and on three levels: cosmic, corporate, and personal. The first obviously serves as the greatest display of God's might. This means that any description of God's power must begin in the opening verses of the Bible: "In the beginning God created the heavens and the earth" (Gen. 1:1). God's unrivaled power is on full display from the opening verse. From the primordial nothingness, he caused energy and matter to erupt into existence at his command. With no pre-existent materials with which to work, he executed the divine blueprint for a sprawling universe that can only cause his creatures to marvel in wonder, yet it is stamped with the imprint of its Maker (cf. Rom. 1:18). Through the prophet Jeremiah he asks, "Is anything too hard for me?" (Jer. 32:27). Obviously this is a rhetorical question!

The origin of time highlights the creative effort of God. Before then, there was no world, no heavenly bodies, and no physical matter whatsoever. The basis of this claim is the use of the Hebrew word *bara'*, meaning to "create." While there are several words the Old Testament uses for the creation of something, only *bara'* is used of God. The other terms are used by both God and man, but all mean to fashion or shape something from pre-existent material. Man is never spoken of as creating something from nothing.

It is difficult to imagine the power of a great number of things. If someone has never fired a handgun, it is difficult for that person to estimate the recoil the weapon will produce. The destructive power of a nuclear weapon is beyond the imagination of many people. What about the sun, a giant nuclear reactor the size of thousands of Earths? What about the power that it takes to bring that sun, and the other 200 billion other stars like it in our universe, into existence? That takes the power of God.

The release of power usually takes some kind of exertion, but this is not the case with God. Imagine the incredible power needed to create a universe, and then consider the fact that that universe was created effortlessly. God merely spoke the words, and his creation appeared. At his command the stars, planets, and other heavenly bodies blink into existence. He wished there to be animals and plants upon the earth, and it was so. God created absolutely everything (Heb. 1:2; 11:3).

While he shows his might on the cosmic level through creation, he also demonstrates it on the corporate level with his people. One particularly note-worthy case is the Exodus from Egypt. It has been called the "gospel of the Old Testament," and for good reason. It was the greatest episode of the deliverance of a people in the ancient world.

During the time of Moses, Egypt was one of the superpowers of the ancient Near East. It had the most powerful military at the time, and it ruled not only Egypt, but much of Palestine as well. During this time it was believed that wars were fought on two levels: the human and the divine. Human affairs were largely determined by the gods, and whichever side had the most powerful gods would win. With Egypt ruling substantial territory in the Near East and the Hebrews serving as slaves, it was clear to the man on the street which side had the most powerful gods. When Moses meets with the king, Pharaoh is no doubt suspicious of this Hebrew deity. Pharaoh does not know who He is and does not appear to care. But God knows how to show his power to his people and to the Egyptians, and it all comes to a head in the showdown of the century.

The Ten Plagues is the story not only of catastrophic disasters on the Egyptians, but also of the triumph of Yahweh over their gods. Not every plague targets a specific deity, but it does affect the areas of reality that the Egyptian gods were thought to govern. The plagues of flies and frogs that rage out of control probably targeted the various fertility gods, who could not keep the animals in check. The plague of hail probably targeted the sky god Nut, who could not prevent it from destroying the Egyptian crops. The plague of darkness was aimed at the various sun gods of Egypt, several of whom were thought to have been exceptionally powerful. In every case, God is able to demonstrate the impotence, and therefore the non-existence, of the Egyptian deities. Many years later, even the Philistines are aware of the monumental victory of Yahweh. Mistakenly believing that the Hebrews served many gods like they did, they cry out, "Woe to us! Who can deliver us from the power of these mighty gods? These are the gods who struck the Egyptians with every sort of plague in the wilderness" (1 Sam. 4:8).

The third way in which God demonstrates his power is on the personal level. We find the signs and miracles in the Bible that demonstrate the power of God often do so in accompaniment to revelation. That is, prophets, apostles, and even Jesus himself often performed signs to validate their messages. There is one sign, however, that demonstrates the power of the divine in an intimate way.

Jesus became God incarnate. He was God, but he also experienced the full range of human emotions and experiences. This included having a family. Mary, Martha, and Lazarus were some of his closest friends. One day, Jesus is told that Lazarus is ill. There is little doubt about the relationship between Jesus and Lazarus—he is called the one whom Jesus loves. Surprisingly, Jesus waits before departing to Bethany to see Lazarus.

When Jesus arrives, Lazarus is dead. His friend has been in the grave four days. Everyone he knew was powerless to stop death from claiming its victim. But everyone also knows that Jesus had the power of preventative healing. They tell him, "Lord, if you had been here, my brother would not have died" (John 11:21, 32). This was not a simple expression of sorrow—it may have also been a veiled accusation. Jesus had the power to ward off death itself, but he did not do so. Others asked a similar question: "Could not he who opened the eyes of the blind man also have kept this man from dying?" (John 11:37).

They knew about Jesus' power to heal, but did not expect him to raise the dead. Martha says, "I know that whatever you ask from God, God will give you" (John 11:22), but it apparently did not include a request for Lazarus to rise from the grave. This is clear from her reaction when Jesus asks the other to open the tomb. Martha, like everyone else, may think that Jesus is being unreasonable (John 11:39). Like other Jews of the day, Martha did believe in a corporate resurrection in the future, but she certainly did not think that it would happen anytime soon.

There was no question that Lazarus was dead. Martha is identified as "the sister of the dead man" (John 11:39). Furthermore, Jews believed that the soul of the deceased hovered about the body for three days after death.[1] Notice that Jesus is there on the fourth day—the time at which resurrection was believed impossible. For all practical purposes, Lazarus was dead, and he was not coming back until the day of the Lord when all the faithful would be resurrected sometime in the indeterminate future. Jesus refused to wait that long.

Jesus commands the tomb to be opened and calls for Lazarus to appear. In that demand there is all the authority of an omnipotent God who is turning the natural order on its head. Death is a power that no living thing can escape. It is a creeping doom that inevitably, inexorably, consumes all life. Yet the command of Christ caused it to shrink back and release its hold on Lazarus. Through Christ, humanity can escape the clutches of death.

POWERFUL TO THE EXTREME, BUT NOT TO ABSURDITY

In speaking of God's omnipotence, we often say that he can do absolutely anything. This is not entirely true. It would be more accurate to say that God can do absolutely anything that does not go against his nature or violate his character. There are some things that he definitely cannot do, such as lie, cheat, or steal. He cannot kill himself, nor do anything that is absurd or illogical.

---

1.   See Darrell L. Bock and Gregory J. Herrick, *Jesus in Context: Background Readings for Gospel Study* (Grand Rapids, MI: Baker Academic, 2005), 231.

It is sometimes asked, "Can God create a rock so big that he cannot lift it?" The answer to this question really is not an answer at all, but a recognition that the question itself borders upon the absurd. Should one answer "yes" or "no," the end result is that God is limited in some way. "Yes" means that God can create, but not lift, the stone. "No" means that God is strong, but does not have the power to create something that he is unable to lift. Either way, this question is a catch-22 situation, and it stems from a failure to properly understand what omnipotence truly means.

Some may ask, "Can God make a squared circle?" Anyone asking the question does not realize that the query is absurd. A circle is round, while a square has four straight sides of equal length. If God were to take a circle and square it, the end result would be a square. Likewise, if he were to take a square and make it circular, it would become a circle. As powerful as he is, God cannot do something illogical or absurd. The question to ask such a person is "What does a squared circle look like?" If they can describe it, than obviously God could create it.

Someone may ask, "If God is so powerful, can he create another God?" The answer to this is no, because the second one by definition would be a created being. Since God is not a created being, it would not be possible to create something that is uncreated. This would be an absurd violation of logic.

God is never frustrated by an inability to do something and cannot be prevented from accomplishing his will. He never has to contend with anyone. I remember as a teenager having to spar one night in a karate class. I was a brown belt and was matched up against one of the instructors, a second degree black belt several years older than me. The first one to score five points was the winner. In a matter of seconds, he rang up four unanswered points. I was angry and figured I would lose anyway, but I refused to do it without scoring. I carefully approached and answered with four unanswered points of my own. When it came to the deciding round, I got the last point, winning the match. The instructor was furious that I had won. He was the black belt, the better fighter. He was supposed to win. God never has to make that admission.

SOMETIMES POWER IS RESTRAINT

There is great comfort in knowing the difference between divine power and human power. The old maxim, "Power corrupts, and absolute power corrupts absolutely" is a truism illustrated by countless episodes throughout human history. There is perhaps no better illustration than that of Italian political philosopher Niccolo Machiavelli. Read in history and political science courses in every university in the Western world, Machiavelli's book *The Prince* lays out a strategy for the secular ruler to use in controlling his people. Power is evidenced through control, deception, and a host of other weapons in the political arsenal of the prince. For the medieval ruler influenced by Machiavelli, the iron fist was concealed by a velvet glove, but only just.

God's power is very different from that of Machiavelli's prince. For all of God's might, we also see another side: restraint. We see him bellowing at Job from the whirlwind, but we also see him speaking to Elisha in a small, still voice. We see God's unflagging power in the Ten Plagues of Egypt and the destruction of the Assyrian army camped outside Hezekiah's capital (2 Kings 19). But we also see tenderness in the life of Christ as he healed one person after another. His power may be used against his people when they sin, but he also uses it for their benefit.

We see a side of God that has left thinkers in wonder for two thousand years. We imagine a little stable, most likely a cave, in which a young couple is celebrating the birth of their first child. The mother holds her little boy close despite her exhaustion. The father beams with pride. In this newborn child we see the face of God.

This child would grow up like any other in the rough and tumble world of first-century Palestine. He would be a great teacher, a powerful speaker, and a renowned healer. The masses would love him until he challenged them in their comfort zones. Most would abandon him, including his most valued disciples. His own creation would taunt and ridicule him during his execution.

In the midst of betrayal and unfathomable agony, Jesus could have responded with the full might of a justly and righteously indignant God. The text notes that Christ could have called down twelve legions of angels to rescue him (Matt. 26:53). A Roman legion at full strength had 6,000 soldiers. If one angel was enough to eradicate an Assyrian army of 185,000 men (2 Kings 19:35), how much could 72,000 angels do? Jesus had enough divine firepower at his command to turn planet Earth into a void in space. Instead, he allowed himself to die just as he had allowed his captors to retrieve him from Gethsemane (cf. John 10:18).

PROMISES, PROMISES

Another way God's power is displayed is by the trustworthiness of his promises (cf. Mal. 3:6). If a human being were to make a promise, it is with the understanding that there are conditions that must be met. If it is in the future, the person must still be alive and be able to fulfill that promise. If that person should die or become incapacitated, then the promise cannot be fulfilled. He or she is not powerful enough to ensure that the promise will be kept, and may pass it on to another who will keep it for them afterwards.

God will always be able to carry out his promises at any point in the future. If he were not able, then he would be a gambler, if not a liar. Since he is eternal and infinitely powerful, the conditional element does not apply. Human beings must say, "I will promise to do this if I am able." God says, "I will promise to do this," and nothing can stop it.

While we can take great comfort in the promises of God, and in the knowledge that he is benevolent, we cannot make the mistake of assuming that God is a cosmic push-over. His power can be incredibly disquieting.

Job is remembered as a man with nearly unfathomable patience. He endures his own financial ruination, the deaths of his children, his wife's pleas to curse God and die, and his own friends' accusations that he was suffering only what he had deserved. Throughout the book, Job asks for his day in court. If he could just plead his case before the Almighty, maybe he could get somewhere. Spending chapter after chapter in debate with his friends—and nearly calling God out in the process—Job finally gets what he wants. Or that is what he thinks.

The clouds darken on the horizon. Something strange is afoot. The clouds roll toward Job and his friends with supernatural speed. The wind picks up, and in no time it is roaring in the ears of the terrified men. The atmospheric juggernaut grinds toward the men with such ferocity that each of them falls to his knees in terror. With a blast that knocks them to the ground, they hear the voice of God himself. "Who is this that darkens counsel by words without knowledge?" (Job 38:2).

This divine interrogation is designed to leave Job helpless. He is pelted by one unanswerable question after another. A handful would be bad enough, but Job is asked a total of 64 questions, none of which he can answer. Each one highlights the indescribable power of God in ways that confound the intellect.

> **God's power is an attribute that many confess as immeasurable, but they act quite differently.**

God's power is an attribute that many confess as immeasurable, but they act quite differently. A. W. Tozer once said, "Christianity at any given time is strong or weak depending upon her concept of God. And I insist upon this and I have said it many times, that the basic trouble with the Church today is her unworthy conception of God. ... Our religion is weak because our god is weak."

The self-centered perspective of modern man has influenced Christianity in a highly negative way, perhaps more than many of us might realize. We have taken commandments and turned them into suggestions; we have demoted the Creator to the status of an advisor; we have used our theology to shape the Bible instead of allowing the Bible to shape our theology.

So what do people do in the face of a weak God? Nearly anything. There is far less compulsion to do what is right and far more temptation to do what is wrong. Man feels free to describe what God cannot do. Humanity asserts its autonomy and redefines justice. We take it upon ourselves to retool biblical teaching so that it falls in line with our own preconceived notions of mercy and tolerance. In this upside-down world, man is the master and God is the slave. No wonder many people perceive Christianity as weak. We have put the God of Job in a room marked, "Do Not Disturb" and installed an idol in his place. Ironically, a weak God only makes us look pathetic.

God has made many promises in Scripture. He told Abraham he would be the father of a nation. He told Noah he would never destroy the earth again by flood. He told David that the monarch would have a descendant on the throne forever. He tells humanity—if they choose to become part of his family—they will have a home with him in glory. Promise and power are joined together, so that nothing God says can be overturned by anyone else.

QUESTIONS TO CONSIDER

1. What do the events of Genesis 1-2 indicate about the power of God?

2. Apart from the texts mentioned, what are some other places in Scripture that demonstrate the awesome power of God?

3. What does God's omnipotence say about his promises in Scripture?

4. Since God obviously knows what is best for us, why do some people try to tell him how to run things?

5. How does human will work with God's omnipotence?

6. In what ways do we try to limit God's power?

7. God displays his power in action. Can you think of a way in which God can display his power by inaction?

8. What are the limits to God's power?

CHAPTER FIVE

OMNISCIENCE

In January 1820, the English poet John Keats published his famous poem, "Ode on a Grecian Urn." In the poem he examines an urn depicting a scene of young people at play while musicians strum their instruments in the background. He questions the urn, asking the identity of the individuals on the artifact. What activities are they performing? What kind of melodies are the musicians playing? The urn—the "bride of quietness," as he calls it—is silent, and yet eternal. Thousands of years later, the musicians still play a tune that will never be heard. The youths play on, but their names go unspoken. The location of the town in which they live will never be known. This scene may have once occurred in the ancient world, but the mists of time have concealed its details forever.

Keats' famous urn is joined by a host of other works of art whose subjects are beyond our ability to question. Frescoes from the city of Pompeii show portraits of the inhabitants of the city, sometimes with thoughtful expressions. One famous scene shows a woman with a pen in hand, ready to write something down on a tablet. What is she about to write? Other famous works are just as enigmatic. Why is the figure in Edvard Munch's *The Scream* screaming? What is Rodin's *Thinker* thinking? Why is the *Mona Lisa* smiling?

Humans have an insatiable thirst for knowledge. We want to know everything about how things work and what other people think. Science observes, categorizes, classifies, and quantifies. Scholarship in every discipline pursues knowledge down to the tiniest detail. Yet for all our energy and endeavor in an age where more information is within reach than at any other time in human history, we will never know everything. As the old saying goes, "The more we know, the more we know that we don't know."

NOTHING MORE TO KNOW

Humans seem fascinated with possessing the ability to see things others cannot. Superman had X-ray vision. Fortune-tellers claim to glimpse the future through a crystal ball or in the pattern of tea leaves at the bottom of a teacup. Gamblers use every advantage to forecast who will win the race, the pennant, or the big game. Buyers for clothing stores try to chart the trends and predict what fashion lines will be popular from year to year. We want to know, and yet we can know nothing in the future with certainty.

Sharply contrasting with the limitations of human knowledge is that of God. Scripture portrays God as supreme in every way, including his ability to know. God's ability to know is described as omniscience, which comes from the terms *omni* ("all") and *sciens* ("knowledge"). It describes the fact that God knows everything there is to know, and he never needs to ask any questions.[1] No fact or detail escapes him, and he has no need to go to school, read the paper, or watch the news.

God's omniscience means that there is nothing he cannot know. This includes not only all brute facts, but opinions and thoughts as well. He knows all three phases of human time: past, present, and future. Humans can know the past and

---

1.   By this we mean questions to gain information. God often asks questions in the Bible, but they are either rhetorical or are intended to get humanity to think or realize something (much like parents often do).

present in limited ways, but we can only speculate about the future. Unlike us, God knows all things in all possible ways.

God knows everything, and he cannot forget anything. The human mind is prone to forgetfulness. We are amazed by those who have eidetic or photographic memories, who can remember with clarity virtually anything they see. We tend to forget or misremember. There is no better example of this than asking an adult male about his high school football career. In his mind, the sports enthusiast goes from a third-string water boy to a state championship quarterback. We have a way of distorting facts through misperception and by influence of emotion.

STOP STARING AT ME

People can be very private creatures. We do not like others knowing our business. Deep down inside, we have reservations about being known too well or being too predictable. Reputations are protected like gold. Our past is a precious thing, and for some, keeping it hidden is something worth dying for.

The French philosopher Jean-Paul Sartre was incredibly uncomfortable with the idea of an all-knowing, all seeing-God. As a well-known figure, Sartre must have been accustomed to people noticing him in public. But unlike the casual observer in a corner café, God is all-seeing—a "cosmic eye"—who scrutinizes every fiber of each human being. The discomfort for Sarte was not the thought of being examined, but that the examination itself reduced the person to the status of an object, much like a visitor touring a museum to view the great works of art. The tourist could view each piece, carefully examining each curve of the statue, each brush stroke of the painting. In doing so, the observer was ultimately examining an object. Sartre felt this is what God does to the human being. His penetrating vision reduces the human being to nothing more than a piece of living sculpture, one of many pieces in his collection in the museum called Earth.

Although an atheist, Sartre's view of the vision of God is still a disturbing one. We prize our privacy. We conceal ourselves with curtains and blinds, tinted windows, and privacy fences. According to psychologists, we each have a two- to three-foot bubble of "personal space." Whenever someone intrudes into that space, we speak of it as an invasion or violation. We do not like it when someone looks at us for an extended period of time. We like our privacy, and are willing to spend money to maintain privacy when possible.

In one sense, there is something wonderful about God's inescapable vision, especially when we consider the problem of evil. God's sweeping vision means that no crime goes without a witness, and no injustice eludes detection. For every crime that happens on earth, there is a divine witness who is faultless. His testimony is irrefutable, his character unimpeachable. He is the one witness who can never be biased or get confused or forgetful. On that wonderful and terrible day of judgment (Rom. 14:10; cf. 1 Cor. 4:5), there is no defense when God takes the witness stand.

THE GOD WHO HOLDS THE FUTURE IN HIS HANDS

No human being knows what is going to happen five minutes from now. We have assumptions and expectations. We can even offer reasonable predictions or approximations, but certainty of the future is something that we do not have. God sees all of human history in a single glance. In the academic world, however, there is some disagreement over what God can know. The major issue is the question "Can God know the future?"

Christians have claimed that God knows everything, including the past, present, and future. There is a challenge to this claim called open theism. The view states that God can only know what can be known—which excludes the future, since it has not happened yet. He is omnipresent, so he knows everything that has ever happened or is happening now. God has to keep up with current events just like everybody else.

While open theism is an attractive alternative for some theologians,[2] it is far from helpful. The God who does not know the future is not a God who is master of his creation. It borders upon the ridiculous to claim that Yahweh created the universe yet has no idea where it is headed or what it is going to do.

Predictive prophecy is particularly thorny for open theism. Let us consider the example of Joseph. He receives dreams of greatness that indicate one day his family will bow down to him. But what about the moment when his brothers plot against him and sell him into slavery? Here, the God who does not know the future is working furiously behind the scenes, trying to salvage the situation. He is literally trying to make Joseph's dreams come true, or else he runs the risk of being labeled a liar. How relieved God must be when he finally pulls it off!

The ultimate experience is that of Christ. If God could not know the future, Christ's mission would have been utterly ridiculous. God could not have known that his Son would pass the test every time he was tempted. Christ was tested in every way that other human beings are (Heb. 4:15), yet committed no sin. How could God have been sure of this? He must have been wringing his hands for over thirty years, hoping every second of every moment that Jesus would not fall into sin. He made the biggest gamble in the history of the world and hit the biggest jackpot ever won.

Open theists believe that the all-knowing God of Christian theology comes from parallels in Greek literature. This is a popular assertion, but it overlooks the fact that the Greek gods did not possess unlimited knowledge. It also ignores Old Testament passages about God's knowledge. For instance, God knows what we will pray (Isa. 65:24; Matt. 6:8). This is not just an astute observation given the facts, with God serving as a kind of divine Sherlock Holmes. It is a genuine foreknowledge of the future.

---

2.   For the argument in favor of open theism, see John E. Sanders, *The God Who Risks: A Theology of Divine Providence*, 2nd ed. (Downers Grove, IL: InterVarsity Press, 2007). For the argument against, see Bruce A. Ware, *Their God is Too Small: Open Theism and the Undermining of Confidence in God* (Wheaton, IL: Crossway, 2003).

The prophet Isaiah makes other statements concerning God's foreknowledge. In presenting a charge to the pagan gods, God tells them to declare the future, that all might know that they are truly genuine (Isa. 41:22-23; cf. 46:9-10). God identifies knowledge of the future as a basic attribute of divinity. For the false gods to even be considered divine, they must display foreknowledge. In two speeches, the prophet challenges the gods of the nations to demonstrate their abilities and prove their worth. He says,

> Let them bring them, and tell us what is to happen. Tell us the former things, what they are, that we may consider them, that we may know their outcome; or declare to us the things to come. Tell us what is to come hereafter, that we may know that you are gods; do good, or do harm, that we may be dismayed and terrified. Behold, you are nothing, and your work is less than nothing; an abomination is he who chooses you. (Isa. 41:22-24)

Isaiah challenges the "nothings" to a test of deity by declaring what is to happen in the future. In a later passage, the prophet says,

> Thus says the Lord, the King of Israel and his Redeemer, the Lord of hosts: "I am the first and I am the last; besides me there is no god. Who is like me? Let him proclaim it. Let him declare and set it before me, since I appointed an ancient people. Let them declare what is to come, and what will happen. Fear not, nor be afraid; have I not told you from of old and declared it? And you are my witnesses! Is there a God besides me? There is no Rock; I know not any." (Isa. 44:6-8)

The Messianic prophecies concerning Jesus are guarantees that God does indeed know the future. It would be almost dishonest for God to make claims that he is uncertain will come to pass. Jesus knew that Judas would betray him (John 6:64), was aware of the major details in Peter's life before they happened (cf. Mark 14:30; John 21:18-19), and foretold the destruction of the Temple nearly forty years prior to the event (Matt. 24:2).

There are passages that some scholars feel imply that God is not all-knowing. In Genesis 3:9, God calls out to the man, "Where are you?" God was not asking where Adam would be, but rather for Adam to identify his present location. This does not imply a limit to God's knowledge. During the episode when God is asking questions, he is not doing so because his knowledge is deficient; he asks in order to make the couple consider what they have done. It is no different than a parent asking a child what he has done when his activity is obvious. It is a tool for getting the child to own up to his or her actions.

In Genesis 11, human beings have begun building a city and a tower. Defying God's commands to fill the earth, they decide to remain in one place and make a name for themselves. God announces that he will go down to see what the people are doing. Is he surprised at their defiant actions? No, more likely the author of Genesis is stressing that God is minimizing the importance of the building effort. Instead of making a tower reaching up to the heavens, the Lord goes down to take a closer look at the tiny building. It shows their efforts to be what they really are: the pitiful construction of a puny people who think much more highly of themselves than they ought.

GOD IS NO FOOL

Bad report cards can feel like death warrants. Occasionally, they get lost — rather conveniently in the cases of students who have performed exceptionally poorly. It leads some children to make up stories where they went. In 2011, an eleven-year-old boy faked his own kidnapping in order to avoid bringing home his report card. He concocted a story about escaping from a man who threatened him with a pistol, claiming the man was going to kill him. The boy told his family that he leaped to safety from the vehicle, leaving his book bag behind. Soon after the police became involved, he confessed. His grandfather had to call the police and apologize. The authorities were already suspicious of the story, because the boy was able to escape with his band instrument but not his book bag.[3]

It is difficult to conceal the truth, and some do it better than others. I had my own near-apocalyptic experience with a bad report card once, but I was slightly more devious than the boy from Alabama. This particular report card was easily the worst I had ever received, and I was terrified as I tried to come up with an explanation. Then a brilliant scheme came to mind. Our report cards were sent on printouts. All I had to do was cut out good grades from a previous report card and carefully paste them over the bad ones. I deliberately chose grades that did not look too good so it would not draw any suspicion. It took nearly an hour, but it was perfect. All I had to do was choose my moment.

I waited a couple of days before the perfect opportunity presented itself. It was a rainy day, and we usually did not have many lights on in the house during the daytime. My mother was mopping the floor of our darkened foyer. I made my move. Busy with chores in a dimly lit room, she never stood a chance. She looked at my grades and complimented me, but made sure to tell me I could do better as she handed back the doctored report card. I went away happily, pleased to have escaped whatever medieval torture I'm sure I would have suffered had the truth been known.

It is one thing to fool another person, and something else entirely to fool ourselves, especially where relationships are concerned. There are countless people stuck in bad relationships with partners who take them for granted or abuse them. Despite the ill treatment they suffer, these poor souls offer a variant of the same explanation: "I know he takes me for granted/ignores me/abuses me, but I know he still loves me." Should they threaten to leave or break off the relationship, the offender offers a token gift, gesture, or commitment to worm their way back into their partner's good graces. God is not so easily fooled. He does not play

---

3. Steve Campbell, "Boy Fakes Kidnapping to Shed Bad Report Card." *The Huntsville Times*. Online: http://blog.al.com/breaking/2009/09/boy_fakes_kidnapping_to_shed_b.html. Accessed 16 February, 2011.

sentimental favorites or suffer from unhealthy emotional attachments. He knows the heart of every person and is not deceived by cheap gifts meant to purchase a temporary measure of redemption.

Darkening the door of a church every few months, putting a check in the collection plate, or doing a good deed here or there does not register on God's radar. He is not the moonstruck girlfriend who believes with all her heart that her callous, noncommittal boyfriend really does care in spite of every indication otherwise. God does not fall for counterfeit affection that demonstrates love solely for the purpose of achieving a selfish goal. The old saying, "Nice guys finish last" is, unfortunately, all too true. But sometimes that nice guy is God, and he never finishes last. Rather, he always knows the truth in our hearts. Always.

> **Understanding the breadth and depth of God's knowledge should spur us on to greater sincerity and commitment.**

Understanding the breadth and depth of God's knowledge should spur us on to greater sincerity and commitment. Not because we fear him, but because we know he cares. He wants a relationship with his creation. In the Sermon on the Mount, Jesus tells his audience that they should not worry because God knows them and their needs (Matt. 6:25-34). Their futures rest safely in God's hands, whether it is the need for food and clothing in the here and now, or the need for redemption from sin for our life in eternity. God knows everything that people need, and has orchestrated history accordingly to provide those necessities. This was demonstrated in God's provision for the redemption of man 2,000 years ago, one dark day on a hill called Golgotha.

QUESTIONS TO CONSIDER

1. Some people like to be open; others are more private. What is your

response to the fact that God knows you exhaustively?

2. Is it comforting or disturbing to know that God knows everything we do?

3. What is the value to admitting something to God if he already knows it?

4. What does it mean to you knowing you cannot hide anything from God?

5. Are there any limits to God's knowledge?

6. Can God choose to forget something? Why or why not?

7. How would your life be different if you knew what was going to happen a day ahead of time?

8. If God already knows the future, why pray?

CHAPTER SIX

HOLINESS

Everyone is afraid of something. It is only natural to be afraid of certain things, and some fears are more popular than others. Death is usually #1 in the polls. Others include the fear of heights, rodents, and anything involving the number thirteen. Some fears are justified; others can be quirky. Individualistic fears, such as peculiar phobias, can be humorous for those who do not suffer them. I once worked at a restaurant where a fellow employee told me that she was afraid of Styrofoam. Since almost everything was served in Styrofoam cups, she did not last very long.

Some fears are so common to man they are nearly universal. Others are not, but should be. One fear that most do not have is a fear of God, even though "the fear of God" is a common phrase understood by many. Sometimes parents may tell their children they are going to "put the fear of God" into them. In generations past, offensive behavior might be confronted by the question, "Don't you fear God?"

There are things that rightfully make people afraid, and these fears are healthy. God should be feared, but that doesn't mean that we should be afraid of him. One may have a healthy fear of him that includes a dimension of awe and respect for his power and authority. This is the same respect that a child might have for a father and mother. The child does what is asked of him because he not only wishes to avoid punishment, but also because he wants to please his parents and avoid disappointing them.

There is another kind of fear that is held by the person living under a regime of terror. The average person in George Orwell's *1984* was terrified to say anything negative about the government for fear that secret police may whisk them away under the cover of night, never to be seen again. This nightmare was a reality in the former Soviet Union, where something as simple as telling a joke at the government's expense could earn someone a years-long sentence to a labor camp in Siberia. Thankfully, the kingdom of God is not a totalitarian state.

HOLY, HOLY, HOLY

The holy nature of God is both wonderful and terrifying. It is supremely wonderful because of his unsurpassed goodness and purity. In him, we see the ultimate perfection of the craftsmanship within ourselves because we are created in his image. At the same time, God's holiness is a seemingly unendurable force that "evokes trauma and dread."[1] The quality of God's unique moral perfection is portrayed as lethal to those who are imperfect (Exod. 33:20).

The prophet Isaiah came face to face with the terrifying reality of God's holiness (Isa. 6:1-7). Isaiah found himself standing in the throne room of God, and that must have been a spectacular sight to behold. Enveloped in glory in a palace of light, he looks up to see the seraphim flying about overhead, singing praises to God's glory. These majestic and noble beings have two wings with which to fly, another two to cover their feet, and another two to cover their faces. Why must they cover their eyes? The prophet soon finds out.

---

1.   Nahum M. Sarna, *Exploring Exodus: The Origins of Biblical Israel* (New York: Schocken Books, 1996), 45.

His eyes trace the majestic train of God's robe as it fills the temple. His eyes blink, and he instinctively ducks his head as the booming voice of God rattles the solid stone architecture. He sees the smoke from the incense curling upward into the air. Then he sees something that makes his blood run cold. A yawning pit opens up in his stomach and nausea overtakes him. His legs grow weak; his knees buckle. He has seen God with his naked eyes—a privilege afforded only to angels.

In his distress, Isaiah cries out and calls down a curse from heaven upon himself: "And I said: "Woe is me! For I am lost; for I am a man of unclean lips, and I dwell in the midst of a people of unclean lips; for my eyes have seen the King, the LORD of hosts!" (Isa. 6:5). He pronounces a woe—a curse—on himself because he has entered into the presence of God as a sinful man. Moses saw only a part of God (Exod. 33:23), which was enough to cause his face to glow with the radiance of God's glory, and this was enough to cause the people to tremble in fear. The prophet Isaiah, as a great man of God familiar with the Torah, knew that his own fears were well-founded. Moses got the equivalent of a divine suntan. Isaiah walked into the heart of a supernova.

The apostle John had a similar reaction. When confronted by Christ, appearing among the seven golden lampstands "like a son of man," John "fell at his feet as though dead" (Rev. 1:13, 17). The apostle whom Jesus loved likewise understood the wonder and terror of God's holiness, and that Jesus being One with the Father (John 10:30) shared in that holiness. John's actions should tell us something about the respect and awe that Christ commands.

There are other examples of this behavior in the Bible. In Judges 13, Manoah and his wife are visited by an angel of the Lord. They offer to feed the angel, whom they think is a man. He does not eat, telling them to offer a sacrifice instead. After he ascends in the flame of the altar upon which they are making the offering, Manoah realizes that this man was actually God. With this realization they fall to the ground on their faces. Manoah proclaims, "We shall surely die, for we have seen God" (Judg. 13:22). Gideon has a similar experience, and must be comforted by God: "Peace be to you. Do not fear; you shall not die" (Judg. 6:23).

Common to all of these instances is that once the people realize that they are in the presence of God, they exhibit a pattern of self-abasement. Either the individual falls down prostrate or cries aloud that his or her doom is sure for having seen God. Holiness makes God an object of awe and admiration, but also one of fear and dread. We are to love God with all our being, yet this God is one whose purity cannot tolerate sin in his presence (Hab. 1:13). While God loves his people and has plans for their prosperity (Jer. 29:11), he will not sit idly by while they impinge upon his holiness. God is a loving Father, but he is also an impartial Judge and a mighty Warrior.

Holiness is perhaps God's most fundamental attribute.[2] Everything about him is holy. It is an integral part of all he is and does. There is nothing about God which is not governed by his holiness. He loves with a holy love, dispenses justice with holy judgment, and burns with holy wrath.

Even those who are the people of God cannot know what it is to be completely undefiled, without sin, and pure in every thought and deed. Such things are beyond the scope of our limited abilities because God is so uniquely holy (1 Sam. 2:2; Exod. 15:11; Isa. 40:25). It is difficult to think of an approximation when the item in question is so foreign that we can only understand it in part.

In the Old Testament, the term "holy" refers to that which is distinct or set apart for special purposes. The root in Hebrew is *qadosh*, meaning "be holy" or "set apart." God is distinct and decidedly "other," different from everything he creates. That which is holy is sharply contrasted with what is not; the two were not to be confused. It carries with it the vertical dimension of supremacy. The name of God is not like any other; it is a holy name (Lev. 22:32; Psa. 145:21; Ezek. 20:39). The Holiest of Holies was no ordinary room; as the innermost room of the temple, it was a place where none could venture except for very special circumstances. Those items belonging to the Temple that were consecrated for special use were not to be utilized for ordinary purposes.

---

2. Gerald Bray, *The Doctrine of God* (Downers Grove: InterVarsity Press, 1993), 215.

In the New Testament, we see something of the holy nature of God. The word used is *hagios*, which has similar meaning to its Old Testament counterpart. Though it occurs infrequently, it does echo and reinforce what is seen in the Old Testament. For instance, God is called thrice holy in Isaiah's vision (Isa. 6:3), with this unparalleled declaration of God's holiness (called the *Trisagion*) being repeated by the four living creatures in Revelation 4:8. Elsewhere, God is labeled as holy several times (John 17:11; 1 Pet. 1:15; Rev. 6:10). This term is applied to his name (Luke 1:49), covenant (Luke 1:72), prophets (Luke 1:70), law (Rom. 7:12), and the Scriptures (Rom. 1:2). The word is also applied to Christ, who is called the "Holy One of God" (Mark 1:24; Luke 4:34; Acts 3:14) and God's "holy servant" (Acts 4:27).

Ultimately, whether in the Old Testament or New, the basic idea of "holiness" is that of separation. God is separate and distinct from his creation, a fact which lies at the heart of God's relationship to it. He is something other than the created order that he made, and he calls his people to rise above it as well. Sin is responsible for the alienation of humans from God. Only when realizing the gravity of this destructive element do we begin to comprehend the necessity of Christ's saving work. Through his atoning sacrifice, humanity is reconciled to God. While Christians live among the ungodly, the end of time will ultimately see to it that the separation of the godly from the wicked will be swift, sure, and eternal.

A HOLY PEOPLE

The nation of Israel was a people who often disdained the holiness of God. Initially, the Lord called Israel up out of Egypt to serve as a light to the world. Their keeping of the law would serve to show their wisdom and understanding to the surrounding nations, ultimately pointing to God (Deut. 4:6). They were not chosen on the basis of strength, size, or merit, but rather out of God's love in order to be his treasured possession (Deut. 7:6-7). This people, taken from the depths of slavery to serve as God's agent, had to be different and special. They were to denounce the ways of the pagan nations that surrounded them and follow the words of Yahweh exclusively. They had to be holy.

The book of Leviticus arguably says more about holiness than any other book of the Bible. It indicates acts of worship were to be performed "to the Lord." In other words, they were to be performed in the presence of God. Because of his presence in the Most Holy Place, only the high priest was allowed to enter once a year on the Day of Atonement. Those consecrated to be priests had to be free from physical handicap (Lev. 21:17-23). Similarly, the offerings they gave were to be free from blemish or defect (Lev. 1:3).

The laws contained in Deuteronomy also served to show Israel how to act. Their behaviors would be regulated to produce moral and ethical purity in word and deed. The law was such that it mirrored God's nature: the Israelites, if they kept it, would be following the same pattern of behavior that God himself had. They would stand out among the other nations, serving as an example of purity and blamelessness, like God and unlike their neighbors.

Throughout history, sin has been a pervasive element in human behavior. Despite human inability to conquer it, God did not stop from calling his people to be holy. Since they could not be perfectly so, he made a provision for his people to remain holy through sacrifice. It is no different today, though the specifics of the sacrifice made on our behalf are different than those offered in Old Testament times. Ancient Israel offered sacrifices year by year, while Christ made a single offering for humanity (Heb. 10:14). That sacrifice was unblemished (Heb. 9:14), which is what was required by the law (Deut. 15:21). We, too, are called to present ourselves as living sacrifices (Rom. 12:1).

While priests in the Old Testament offered sacrifices brought to them by the people, Jesus offered himself. Only he could be the perfect sacrifice, and only he could offer it. Jesus made history's only perfect act of self-sacrifice. While on earth Jesus told his disciples, "Greater love has no one than this, that someone lay down his life for his friends" (John 15:13). The cross proves that he was truly a man of his word.

Sin is dangerous because it separates us from God. He calls us to be separate from the world, but sinning is nothing short of allegiance to the world and the dark power that rules so much of it. Thus, the Christian must have a degree of introspection, examining not only how his or her actions impact others, but what consequences those actions enact.

MAKING SIN UNCOMFORTABLE

God is wrathful because his holiness demands it. God would not be God if his ordinances were violated with no more response than a shrug of his shoulders. He may choose to bestow mercy, but he also metes out justice. It is not like the justice of mankind, which is limited and may or may not fit the crime. The Lord's judgment is everlasting, and the punishment always fits the crime. Committing sins which have eternal implications bring about eternal consequences.

We have an almost inexhaustible ability to minimize sin. Many times we hear of "white lies," "mistakes," and "little secrets." Sins deemed to be benign may be dismissed as harmless. It ignores the fact that each one is a great evil regardless of whether or not it harms another person. Jonathan Edwards once noted, "Almost every natural man that hears of hell, flatters himself that he shall escape it." Even Christians can be tempted into adopting this mindset.

Even in an increasingly secularized society there seems to be recognition of what is holy, even if it is only in mockery. An atheist friend of mine and I attended the same Christian college. He had attended a Christian high school thanks to his parents, and most of our group of friends attended the same university. He told me a story about one afternoon when he took his new girlfriend, who shared his unbelief, to see where he went to college. When they walked on campus she said, "I'm surprised I didn't burst into flame."

There are many different responses to God. Among unbelievers, it can be expressed by scorn and even disgust. Among Christians, it can take the form of boredom and disinterest. There is little sense of the presence of the holy or the presence of God in worship services, much less in daily living. All too often we assume that the wrathful God of the Old Testament is much different than the benevolent God of the New Testament. Israel's God was one whose justice could command the destruction of cities (Deut. 12:13-18). But for many, he is a God of virtually limitless grace who will pardon any sin as long as the sinner shows at least a meager amount of contrition, regardless of how disingenuous it may be.

> **As we come to a deeper knowledge of God, we should acquire an increasing sense of God's holiness.**

As we come to a deeper knowledge of God, we should acquire an increasing sense of God's holiness. Not everyone does, and this includes some who are biblical scholars. Academicians may be able to translate the Bible from its original languages, talk about the subtle nuances of various doctrinal positions, and dissect heresies with theological language sharper than any scalpel. But for all their intellectual acumen, God remains a cold, distant figure who exercises little influence in their lives. This may have nothing to do with their theology, and everything to do with their hearts. Even the demons have an understanding of God, which causes them to tremble (Jas. 2:19). Demons are much better theologians than any human being and have more experience with the divine, but the difference lies in the impact their beliefs make. They are not moved to worship God and persist in their fear-stricken opposition to him.

> God's holiness is his total, unchanging and dynamic being and character out of which he expresses himself consistently and zealously. The two great corollaries of God's holiness are his love and his wrath. When confronted with purity, righteousness and obedience, God's love goes out in embrace and blessing; when confronted with impurity, rebellion or sin in any of its

forms, it expresses itself in wrath. God's wrath is a necessary as well as a personal response to sin. It is the reaction of his truth and righteousness to what would invalidate them. It is the revulsion of his holy being to what challenges its very existence and threatens to disintegrate his creation at every level.[3]

Many people today operate under the misconception that a holy life is a boring life. To be a Christian means being a goody-two-shoes. But taking pleasure in the holy should not be viewed as lame. In fact, we should see it as a wonderful opportunity. It is our time to give the Creator of the universe the ultimate compliment by striving to be just like him. It is a challenge that calls us to live in a more noble and ethically pristine state close to the heart of God.

QUESTIONS TO CONSIDER

1. Describe God's holiness in your own words.

2. Is holiness merely the lack of sin, or does it involve something else as well?

3. What would your response be if you were standing in Isaiah's shoes?

4. How does God's holiness affect the behavior of individual Christians?

5. How is God's holiness different from ours?

6. Imagine an omnipotent, omniscient, omnipresent deity who was not holy. Would you want to know him? Why or why not?

7. The world seems to love the idea of a God who is less holy and more tolerant. Why?

8. Can a person be a Christian without changing his or her lifestyle to reflect God's holiness?

3. Peter Lewis, *The Message of the Living God: His Glory, His People, His World* (Downers Grove: InterVarsity Press, 2000), 188-189.

CHAPTER SEVEN

LOVE

They say it makes the world go 'round. It has its own national holiday. Some people spend their whole lives looking for it. Some people are lucky in it; others are not. It has inspired light-hearted comedies and heart-rending tragedies. What is it? The best four-letter word of all: *love*.

The English language has a number of words with a bewildering number of uses. The word "love" is like that, given the different ways we use the term. What is love? A feeling of affection? Romantic attraction? A pet name for our significant other? We love hamburgers, ice cream, music, and our favorite football team. We also love people, though in an entirely different manner. We may "love" our favorite food, but we would never marry it.

One way of defining love is simply as the desire to make another person's life better. It could involve doing the little things—small expressions of affection. It may involve a sacrifice as well, as in O. Henry's famous short story "The Gift of the Magi." A young married couple, Della and Jim Young, are poor, but want to give the other a meaningful gift for Christmas. They both sell something that is precious to them in order to purchase a gift they know the other will treasure. Jim sells his grandfather's pocket watch to buy an expensive comb for his wife. Della cuts off her beautiful locks to purchase a gold chain for her husband's watch. Their gifts are rendered useless, but they serve as an enduring reminder of their sacrificial love for each other.

GOD IS LOVE

The Bible portrays God as personal, loving, and intimately involved with his creation. He cares for his people and protects them but is willing to chastise them should they need it. He is not a force; he is a person. John makes it quite clear that God is indeed personal:

> Beloved, let us love one another, for love is from God, and who-ever loves has been born of God and knows God. Anyone who does not love does not know God, because God is love. In this the love of God was made manifest among us, that God sent his only Son into the world, so that we might live through him. In this is love, not that we have loved God but that he loved us and sent his Son to be the propitiation for our sins. Beloved, if God so loved us, we also ought to love one another (1 John 4:7-11).

In speaking about the love of God, we first have to define what love actually is. John describes God's love in an emphatic way. Love is not something that God just does, but it is an essential part of his being. The two are not interchangeable. God is the source of all love, but love is not God. We do not deify love, nor do we lower God to being just an emotion. Used as a verb, it means to delight in or cherish. As a noun, it means affection or fondness.

The kind of love God shows is unlike anything ever seen by mortal man. People in the ancient world thought of their gods in very mortal terms. They loved, of course, but they had their favorites, and they could also be aloof and distant. And their "love" looked a lot like human love, complete with disguise, deceit, lust, and seduction. Zeus had hundreds of women and goddesses he seduced and even raped. In the Roman myths, Cupid shot people with arrows designed to cause them to fall in love. For a god, he was a poor marksman, which made for some tricky situations. The love of these gods was always poisoned with human weakness. Mankind needed to recognize the inferiority of their idols, and experience a true and holy God who could love purely and passionately, but in a way that was both unconditional and holy.

Even in the Old Testament, God's love is emphasized; it is called a covenant of love (Deut. 7:12). Based on this covenant relationship, the Bible teaches that God loves his people as a husband loves his wife (Isa. 54:5-8; Jer. 2:2; Hos. 3:1). This love is manifested through his saving acts, which is most readily seen in the deliverance of Israel from Egypt. Israel was chosen on the basis of God's love (Deut. 7:7-8; 10:15).

God's love was to be imitated by his people. Leviticus commanded them to love their neighbors (19:18, 34), care for the poor (19:9-10), practice honesty (19:11), and respect the elderly (19:13, 15, 32). A concern for the weak was paramount in the Old Testament. God calls Israel to care for the widow, orphan, and stranger in the land, three groups of people whom the dishonest could victimize easily. It is no surprise, then, that the New Testament summarizes the law as placing a premium on love. Both Jesus (Mark 12:28-31) and one of the scribes he questions (Luke 10:25-28) agree that to love both God and other people is the chief aim of the law.

BEING LOVED AND BEING KNOWN

Never is the love of God on display more clearly than at the cross. Jesus comes to earth to be utterly humiliated. As the divinely appointed representative who will make atonement for humanity, he must experience everything that we do. He knows what it means to grow up, to skin his knees as a child, to experience pain, to know sorrow, and to weep.

Jesus knew what it meant to experience sorrow. Joseph disappears from the gospels relatively quickly. It could be that Jesus also knew what it meant to lose a father and be saddled with the responsibility of becoming the man of the house at an early age. Although he would raise Lazarus from the dead, it would only be a matter of time before he would again return to the tomb from which Christ had freed him.

Jesus knew what it meant to be humiliated. Only after the crucifixion do his brothers James and Jude seem to realize who Jesus is. That is not surprising, since everyone else—including the disciples—are in the same position. They assume he is less than who he really is, and are shocked when he performs deeds of power (Matt. 8:27; Luke 5:8). He is the co-creator of everything in existence (John 1:1-14), yet is treated as a simple peasant, whom the authorities would later execute as a criminal.

Jesus knew what it meant to suffer. Through the window of the Gospels, we see him in the Garden of Gethsemane praying under incredible duress (Matt. 26:36-46). After he finishes, he looks towards the Temple Mount at the mob coming for him. The Mount of Olives was not much of a mountain, but more of a gentle slope looking down to the Temple Mount. Jesus had a dozen different ways to escape those coming to arrest him. His disciples must have looked on in disbelief as he watched the mob come closer. They knew why the mob was coming for Jesus, but they do not understand why Jesus just stood there, waiting as his doom approaches.

Jesus knew what it meant to be treated with contempt. Through the eyes of the evangelists, we watch the authorities arrest Jesus and parade him through a kangaroo court full of illegalities as he is beaten, mocked, and scorned. Roman soldiers punch him in the face and push a crown of thorns down onto his head. Blood trickles down his forehead and onto his neck and shoulders. He is beaten with scourges, opening gaping wounds in his back, and he is dressed in a robe, given a scepter, and subjected to mock homage. The robe is taken off, and like cloth stuck to a cut, it tears away from the raw skin and reopens his wounds.

We see a cosmic tragedy, watching the co-creator of the universe tortured by his own creation.

Jesus knew what it meant to die. We see him carrying the rough-hewn beam of his cross on shoulders shredded by the Roman scourge. He struggles toward Golgotha, his shuffling footsteps stirring up dust that clings to the tacky blood that covers his skin. The Roman soldiers nail his hands to the cross, severing nerves in his wrists that make it feel as though his arms were on fire. His feet are nailed to the wood, probably by his heels. Every move he makes hits a raw or severed nerve or digs into an open wound.

Love and agony join together in terrible beauty. Jesus once told the disciples "Greater love has no one than this, than to give his life for a friend" (John 15:13). Truly spoken, indeed. After hours of indescribable suffering, he digs up his last reserve of strength and cries out to the God of heaven and earth. The greatest injustice ever committed by the cruelty of man is complete.

It is one thing to see an act of injustice. It is something quite different to see that action taken against a child, especially if that child is ours. The love of God for his creation is demonstrated in his willingness to allow it to abuse and murder his Son. Jesus was made into a mockery, beaten savagely, and finally nailed to a tree and left to die one of the most horrific deaths ever devised. And yet God had to allow his Son to die for humanity so that we might be saved. Even the slightest injustice committed against a child is enough to elicit an angry, perhaps even violent, response from a parent. But the anger of a human is nothing compared to the anger of God. I am supremely thankful that he shows more restraint than we do.

ARE YOU ALL RIGHT?

The remarkable nature of God's love is explained by the parable of the prodigal son. In Luke 15:11-24, Jesus tells the story of a young, arrogant, ungrateful upstart who asks for his inheritance before his father has even died. In the Jewish culture of

Jesus' day, this was tantamount to saying, "I wish you were dead already." The father hands the boy his portion of the inheritance, which is quickly frittered away on frivolities and carnal pleasures. After the money runs out, so do the boy's associates. Deep pockets tend to attract friends; it is another story when the money runs dry.

The spendthrift, out of cash, can only get a job feeding pigs. He is broke and both physically and ceremonially unclean. After realizing that the animals he feeds live better lives than him, he returns home to beg for a job. Being a slave in a mansion is better than being king of a pigpen.

Surprisingly, we see the father scanning the horizon for his son. No doubt wisely aware that those with the personality of his son usually find ways to ruin themselves, he is awaiting the return of the prodigal. The father knows it is only a matter of time, and the son does not disappoint. But that is the point of it all—the father knows his son will wise up and return home. When he spies his son in the distance, the father races at breakneck speed toward him. The son has been practicing his lines, trying to find just the right way to beg for his father's forgiveness. Before he can even begin to grovel, the man cuts him off and immediately calls for a feast. Despite the terrible things he has said and done, the boy still has a place at the father's table. With God, this story is a reality for humanity.

God already knows us and accepts us. When I visited the campus where my wife attended university, I met a motivational speaker she had known while in college. His name was Willie Franklin, but he introduced himself as "Uncle Chocolate." Willie had played in the NFL as a wide receiver for the Baltimore Colts. When I met him, he looked me over like he was buying a new car, squinty-eyed scowl and all. He approached me and asked, "You all right?" I said, "Yeah ... umm, I think so." After looking me over to make sure that I passed muster, he said with a smile, "You're all right."

What if I had not been "all right"? What if I failed to meet with Uncle Chocolate's approval? I never had to worry about it. The same goes with God. By virtue of his omniscience, God knows us better than we will ever know ourselves. He numbers each hair on our heads. He knows the exact count of how many cells are in our bodies. He knows every choice we will ever make, but he also knows our hearts. The apostle Paul describes the wondrous love of God by saying, "While we were enemies we were reconciled to God by the death of his Son" (Rom. 5:10). God knew the deepest recesses of our hearts and the darkest secrets hidden within them. Despite our ability to sin with nauseating regularity, God sent his Son to suffer for us.

LOVING GOD

Because God loves us, we are expected to love God in return. John tells his readers that "anyone who does not love does not know God, because God is love" (1 John 4:8). Jude urges his readers to remain in God's love (Jude 21). Paul notes that of the three Christian virtues—faith, hope, and love—the latter is the greatest (1 Cor. 13:13). We have been the recipients of God's love, so we must love others in return. Christ laid down his life on our behalf, so we must be ready to do the same (1 John 3:16).

Aristotle once said, "One cannot love whom he fears." We talk about having a fear of God. Can we both love and fear him at the same time? After all, it seems impossible to have a personal relationship with someone we keep at arm's length.

The fear of God is not to be afraid of him, but to be afraid to disappoint him. I knew a fellow who once said that if he were granted one wish, he would wish that every human being could sin only once. That way, no human being could arrogantly boast of his or her own goodness, and the plan of God would not be overturned. It was the fear of disappointing God that drove him to obedience.

It is commonplace in our culture to overemphasize the love of God. Many who are

> **The fear of God is not to be afraid of him, but to be afraid to disappoint him.**

professing believers earnestly think that God does not challenge or punish sin. To do this is not loving, they say. They want a God who is kind and benevolent. This may seem like a natural reaction, since human beings tend to fear punishment and wrath. But what these people have done is reduce God to a being of a more manageable size. He no longer has the power to punish evil, and he cannot confront them in wrongdoing. But this God is not really God. This is a counterfeit, a fake, an idol.

THE DRAMA OF REDEMPTION

The drama of redemption is a story that incorporates all the elements of a true love story. There is a God, who is intimately concerned with his creation. He creates mankind, male and female, who betray him. They abandon their God, who expends a tremendous effort to defend the people from sin, from the devil, and from even themselves. He sends his own Son, who pays the ultimate price for those whom he loves. The story of Christ's sacrifice is one of both tragedy and triumph. In the end, death and the devil are defeated. Christ reigns supreme as the King of kings and the Lord of lords, and his people are his own once again.

God's love is constant, even though our sin violates his holy character. This is clearly seen in the book of Hosea. The prophet is told to take a wife in a marriage that will symbolically mirror the relationship between God and his people. Gomer is unfaithful to her husband and eventually sells herself into slavery. An equally vital part of the story concerns the children, who take names illustrating important points about the relationship between Israel and God.

The first child is a boy named Jezreel. The valley of Jezreel would be the place where God would break Israel's military power. The second child was a daughter named Lo-Ruhamah ("not loved"). No longer would God have compassion on his people. The last child was Lo-Ammi; his name means "not my people." Israel had pushed her God to the limit and distanced herself from him. As a result, God would no longer claim his people as his own, effectively disowning them.

But God's forgiving love would not let Israel go forever. After Gomer sells herself into slavery, God tells Hosea to buy her back. The names of the children would be changed to reflect the new status of Israel. The negative aspect of the last two children's names would be dropped. Instead of "not loved," Israel would just be "loved." Instead of "not my people," Israel would be his once again. At the end of the book, God promises great things. He says that he will heal the backsliding of the people and love them freely. They would no longer feel the burning anger of God, but his blessing.

God's love is very much like that of man, but it is also very different. His love is timeless and utterly reliable. It does not stoop to be insulted by pettiness. He loves his people with a love that fulfills his promises and commitments. God's love does not die or grow cold. It is forever fresh, from everlasting to everlasting. From the prodigal son to the prostitute Gomer, God's love pursues his people and refuses to let them go.

QUESTIONS TO CONSIDER

1. How should God's love be reflected in our lives?

2. What are some personal benefits to understanding the love of God?

3. How do our personal failures and shortcomings affect God?

4. In Jeremiah 18 when the potter (representing God) finds that the clay is unusable, he reshapes it into something else. What might this say about the life of the Christian?

5. What are some reasons why a person might feel forsaken by God?

6. Think about the fact that God has known each of us from eternity past. What does that say about his love for us?

7. God disciplines those he loves (Heb. 12:6). Does this mean God *punishes* the ones he loves, or is something else being said?

CHAPTER EIGHT

GOODNESS

Superman is one of the most recognizable figures in the American consciousness. Often called the "big blue Boy Scout" in the comics, Superman represents the noblest features of humanity: concern for others, commitment to justice, and devotion to the idea of the sanctity of life. Originally conceived as a mythic champion of social justice under the shadow of the Great Depression, his exploits have been enjoyed by millions over the past seventy years, whether on the radio, in print, or on the silver screen.

Despite his popularity today, most people would not recognize the Superman of the 1930s. Most people think of the character as a bastion of morality devoted to truth, justice, and the American way. What many people do not realize is that the earliest incarnation of Superman featured a rough, flawed hero quite unlike the one we know today. His treatment of villains would be shocking to modern audiences. In the earliest portrayals, he uses threats, scare tactics, and physical violence to frighten villains and force them into compliance. He seems unconcerned with throwing his opponents about in a manner that would easily result in fatalities, although they were not explicitly shown. In one story, Superman beats up a gangster, then throws him into the line of fire when other gangsters begin shooting at him. Thankfully, one of the early editors quickly gave Superman the sterling code of conduct he retains today.

At the dawn of the 21st century, good guys are becoming scarce. It seems our society is taken with the idea of the anti-hero, the protagonist who has severe shortcomings with a sprinkling of redeeming qualities. It is increasingly common for heroes to be seen as regular people, complete with their own failings ranging from substance abuse to outright moral indecency. No matter how good, power-ful, or noble, even heroes have their imperfections. We like it that way because we do not want to feel inferior. We want to be saved, but we do not want to feel badly for it. We like our heroes to be good, but not too good.

THE GOODNESS OF GOD

The goodness of God seems to be one of his more underrated attributes. The most notable stories of the Bible usually revolve around the themes of judgment, sorrow, or triumph over evil and suffering. We think of the ferocity of his wrath, the greatness of his mercy, and the depths of his love. Goodness does not generate great wonder or fascination.

In our culture, it is not enough to say that something is simply "good," es-pecially in advertising. In order for something to sell, it has to be "better" or "im-proved." Sometimes the very fact that something is "new" will satisfy the appetite of the every-hungry American consumer. It seems that unless we attach some fantastic adjective to what we are talking about, it really does not seem all that great after all. Good is too blasé, too boring.

We may speak of God's goodness in two ways. First of all, he is good. Good-ness describes his being and character. He is supremely good: nothing and no one else is better, nor can they be his equal (Luke 18:19). God is perfectly good, so he can never be any better, nor can he get any worse. The psalmists never seemed to tire of celebrating God's goodness (Psa. 25:8; 34:8; 86:5; 100:5; 135:3). Puritan

Thomas Manton put it this way:

> God is naturally good. There is such an absolute perfection in his nature and being, that nothing is wanting to it, or defective in it; and nothing can be added to make it better....He is good of himself good in himself....[T]he creatures' good is a superadded quality; in him it is his essence.[1]

Secondly, we may speak of what he does as being good. Not only is he good, that goodness manifests itself in how he acts. All he does is worthy of approval. He is kind and generous in how he deals with his people, especially the righteous: "No good thing does he withhold from those who walk uprightly" (Psa. 84:11). Since God is by nature a perfectly good being, then obviously he could never commit an evil act. Faithfulness, mercy, grace, and love are all a part of the goodness of God. Betrayal, cruelty, and wickedness are not.

It is interesting that God is good in ways that human beings are not. We like to show kindness to our friends and family, or those we deem worthy. In other words, our goodness is often qualified or restricted in some way. God is good, not only to his own people, but to his enemies as well. "The LORD is good to all, and his mercy is over all that he has made" (Psa. 145:9). Jesus expresses the same idea in the Sermon on the Mount in a different way: "He makes his sun rise on the evil and on the good, and sends rain on the just and on the unjust" (Matt. 5:45). Anyone can return one kindness for another; it takes God to be able to be good even to those who hate him.

CATEGORIES OF GOD'S GOODNESS

Theologians sometimes describe God's attributes in various ways. Since

---

1.   Thomas Manton, *One Hundred and Ninety Sermons on the Hundred and Nineteenth Psalm, Vol. 2* (London: William Bron, 1845), 96.

"goodness" is a fairly broad category, we can break it down into sub-categories: benevolence, love, mercy, and grace.

Benevolence. Benevolence is a simple generosity that God bestows upon all living things. God is the source of every good thing, which includes items we may not normally recognize such as life, rain, and a host of material blessings. Too often we focus on others who live lives of ease. We expect health and wealth without recognizing that sometimes tragedy is an avenue through which God can work to bring blessing (Rom. 8:28). Though God is benevolent to the entire human race, only his people may enjoy his covenant love and fidelity.

Mercy. Mercy is the bestowal of goodness toward those who are in distress, misery, or some other need. God's goodness does not require him to be merciful. That is an added benefit stemming from God's generosity toward his creation. God could vaporize every sinner on the planet and still be a good God; in fact, his goodness requires him to punish sin. Although he owes us nothing, he showers a tenderhearted compassion upon his creation.

Grace. Grace is the demonstration of love toward one who deserves punishment. The wages of sin is death (Rom. 6:23), and all guilty human beings deserve to be executed for their crimes. Paul often refers to the fact that we do not deserve God's grace, but receive it regardless. It is the free and unearned gift of God. We are "justified by his grace as a gift, through the redemption that is in Christ Jesus" (Rom. 3:24).

As Christians we are called to imitate our Creator, not only in holiness, but in goodness as well (3 John 11; cf. Eph. 2:10). Paul instructs the Galatians to "do good to everyone, and especially to those who are of the household of faith" (Gal. 6:10). God is worthy of our love because he is good, which is one of the very reasons for Israel's abundant praise of him in the Old Testament (cf. 1 Chron. 16:34). Goodness is more than an attribute; it is part of his very nature and character.

The wonder of God's goodness is that nothing we do can coerce him to show it regardless of whatever form it may take. It may appear in the forms of mercy, patience, love, kindness, or blessing. On the other hand, human beings may be co-erced into doing virtually anything. Throughout the course of human history when man was at his cruelest, he has forced others to renounce their gods, toil as slaves, and kill their own. They can be made to submit a thousand different ways and provide any number of services under the pain of torture and death. But no human being can be forced to love another. He can be made to show acts of kindness, but they will always be empty of personal feeling or interest. The true tenderness and goodness of man is something that cannot be elicited at the point of a gun.

When God took the people out of Egypt, he told them there is nothing inher-ent in them that caused him to choose them over any of the other peoples of the earth (Deut. 7:7). They were not the biggest, strongest, or most talented. Very little sepa-rated them from the rest of the people in the ancient Near East, apart from one condition: their ancestor Abraham had been given a promise by a merciful and gracious God, and now was the time he chose to make good on that promise. No one forced God to make that promise or to honor it. It is simply in his na-ture to do exactly that.

> **God does not need anything from us, but rather is willing to do everything for us.**

It has been said that the character of a person is revealed in how he treats those who can do nothing for him. No one passes this test like God. His grace is for beggars, the downtrodden, the undesirable. He is willing to serve his people. Jesus tells his disciples that "even as the Son of Man came not to be served but to serve, and to give his life as a ransom for many" (Matt. 20:28). God does not need anything from us, but rather is willing to do everything for us.

When we look at the portrait of God in the Old Testament, we might be tempted to see God as anything but good, especially if we listen to the critics long enough. God is described as an old, cranky, hateful war god who gets no greater pleasure than when throwing down thunderbolts and presiding over the decimation of entire nations. It is true that a lot of judgment takes place in the Old Testament. But what about his goodness? Is there any to be found, especially in the Mosaic Law?

There is a particular focus on God's blessings in the law, but it may not be readily apparent. When we look at covenants from the ancient world, we find that God often patterns the covenants of Scripture after those in use at the time. The covenant at Sinai looks like the covenants made during the mid- to late-second millennium B.C., when Moses lived and the Exodus occurred. Both feature introductions, the history of the two parties making the agreement, and stipulations that the vassals are required to fulfill. Both call witnesses and provide for a deposit of the covenant so that it can be referenced in the future. Likewise, each one features blessings for obedience and curses for disobedience.

There is one difference between the covenant at Sinai and other covenants made at that time that seems significant. In extra-biblical covenants, the curses come first, then the blessings. In the covenant made at Sinai, it is the blessings that come first. While this is a small change, it is an important one. Unlike the gods of the nations who were interested in smiting humans for any and every reason, the God of Israel made it clear that he was more interested in blessing than cursing.

A "GOOD" JUDGE?

Some debate the goodness of God and his Word in an age where all things are permissible and belief is becoming increasingly weak and outdated. Some turn to the Old Testament and see a God of cruelty. Others say that a truly good God cannot co-exist with the evil we see in this world. Scripture is very clear that there is no moral failing in God. There is no darkness in him, no shadow of turning (Jas. 1:17).

Some see the wrath of God as contradicting his goodness. God is unchangeably and perfectly good, so he cannot compromise or negotiate his own goodness. But because of other attributes such as his holiness, justice, and perfection, he cannot allow sin to occur with impunity.

The judge that does not punish where punishment is merited is not just at all. He is an enabler, protecting the criminal from the consequences of crime. This is the very judge some want in God. They want him to overlook sin and display a nearly infinite amount of grace. In reality, God would be foolish in always conceding to our requests, giving us everything we want, never telling us no, and never punishing us for anything. This God is not that good after all.

When God exercises his wrath and righteous judgment, he is being good. He is so good that he cannot allow moral violations to occur without punishment. A person who wants a God that cannot punish is one who wants God to be good whenever it is convenient. It may seem well and good for God to forgive criminals and withhold punishment, but what about the murder victim? What about the woman who has been raped and whose life will never be the same again? Or the child who has been beaten and abused? For the perpetrators to escape punishment is not good, but evil.

GOODNESS, WITH A TOUCH

We see the kindness of God as it touches the lives of human beings in Scripture. In Matthew 8 we read a story of a leper who came to Jesus. He arrives in front of the man called the Christ followed by a multitude of people. The man knew the stories of Jesus, and he had heard of the wondrous deeds this miraculous man was able to do. He kneels in front of Jesus and says simply, "Lord, if you are willing, you can make me clean" (Matt. 8:2-3).

It must have taken courage to kneel before Jesus. Here was a man who had been excommunicated. He was the ultimate reject: jettisoned from the community and shunned by all. His existence was full of despair. Whatever conversation he had with others always began with the same word: unclean (Lev. 13:45)—a continual reminder of his status as an outsider. He likely lived in a colony full of people stricken by a living death that would eventually claim their bodies piece by piece. Hope was a currency that had lost its value long ago.

Jesus does something very important. He not only consents to heal the man, but touches him in order to do so. As a leper, the man would have been able to touch no one, and no one would ever want to touch him. He lived a life completely devoid of physical contact with other human beings. But a tender and powerful touch from the one who helped create the universe and everything in it strips away the disease that had confined him to a torturous prison of rot and decay. All because the God who had become a man took the time to perform a simple act that required no effort on his part, but would change one leper's life forever.

Jesus did not stop with one leper, or even one sinner. All of us have a terminal condition. Every human being is broken and dying. We live in a world that prides itself on its medical acumen, yet it will never find a treatment that can cure our deepest need. Our relationship with God is damaged beyond our ability to repair, and only Christ can heal it. We live a new life not just on this earth, but in eternity, because it is in Christ that we have found the cure for death.

We see God's goodness in the mission of Jesus Christ. His goal, in part, is to demonstrate God's care for his creation. He heals the lame, gives sight to the blind, cures the sick, and raises the dead. These afflictions are unwelcome in God's kingdom. Those whom Jesus healed were a privileged few who were able to enjoy a taste of eternity on earth. One day, the faithful will enjoy it in its fullness forever.

QUESTIONS TO CONSIDER

1. How do we take God's mercy for granted?

2. Does God's goodness mean that the Christian can expect to live life on "easy street"? Explain.

3. God chooses to bless some more than others. Is this unfair? Why or why not?

4. God's grace is a gift we do not earn. Imagine that you are given $1 million to distribute to people in the city where you live. The only stipulation is that none of the recipients has done anything to deserve the gift. How do you determine who will receive the gift?

5. While God's grace is given only to his elect, his goodness is demonstrated to everyone, even those who hate him. Is God wasting his time?

6. What would the world look like if God only demonstrated his goodness to people who trusted in him?

7. In what ways is God's goodness sometimes distorted?

8. Why do you think people in general, including non-Christians, do good things?

CHAPTER NINE

RIGHTEOUSNESS
& JUSTICE

My freshman Bible class teacher walked in one day and spotted one of my classmates chewing a piece of gum. The normal punishment for the offense was two demerits, but the teacher told the student he would receive four instead. My classmate objected, "I thought it is only supposed to be two!" The teacher responded, "I stepped in some gum earlier today, so you get four." The rest of the class laughed, not only because the student was a repeat offender and something of a class clown, but also because few students actually took demerits seriously. But what if it had been a real crime instead of an innocuous misdemeanor? Can a judge increase the severity of a punishment for subjective reasons? Or is there a universal law to ensure justice is fair, dispassionate, and objective?

A perfect being like God is supposed to be righteous and just. A common criticism today is that God is not only unrighteous, but immoral; not only unjust, but cruel. One early heretic named Marcion of Sinope believed that the God of the Old Testament was inhumane and could not be the father of Jesus. Consequently, he edited the New Testament books with a heavy hand, accepting only a pared-down version of Luke, removing Jesus' references to the Father, and removing three of Paul's letters.

The spirit of Marcion is alive and well today. It makes an appearance in the often-repeated phrase, "The God of the Old Testament is a God of wrath; the God of the New Testament is a God of love." Critics are far less kind, saying that God is unjust, cruel, and evil. So what does the Bible have to say? Is God really unjust?

RIGHTEOUSNESS & JUSTICE

We will begin by noting the difference between righteousness and justice. Righteousness is conduct in keeping with moral excellence, while justice means punishing misbehavior according to established law. These two are connected thematically. In Scripture, the standards God sets are not only lawful, but also morally excellent.

We might say that God's righteousness is properly defined as God always acting in accordance with what is right and morally good. Furthermore, he is the ultimate standard of what is right because true righteousness is rooted in his very character. A person may be righteous in a sense, but only as long as he is acting in concert with the will and desires of God. Human beings are not autonomous creatures with the ability to redefine righteousness or introduce new standards by which right living is judged.

Moses writes of God, "All his ways are justice. A God of faithfulness and without iniquity, just and upright is he" (Deut. 32:4). Before Sodom was destroyed, Abraham rhetorically asked God, "Shall not the Judge of all the earth do what is just?" (Gen. 18:25). Like Moses, Abraham knew that God's actions are nothing if not righteous. If God is not righteous, then he is no different than any other god worshipped by men. Pagan gods could do good things. They could also be very, very bad—capriciously so. The difference is that God is morally perfect, and he never acts out of character.

I was sitting in a high school science class as a senior. The teacher was notorious for giving the students a little too much free reign (which, now looking back, was quite a lot of fun, but did not really help because half our class was made up of rebellious students itching for some space to do something bordering on the illegal). One of the students was a junior, and not a very intelligent one at that. He had a particularly rebellious bent that day. When told to sit down so that class could begin, he refused. The teacher, with a much more serious tone, repeated himself while adding the word *now*. This one small word steeled something within my classmate. He defiantly refused to take his seat, and the situation quickly heated. The teacher shoved him down into his seat a couple of times, nearly knocking him on the floor in the process. At a small Christian high school with a teacher who was a professing Christian, I was alarmed. The next day, the teacher offered something resembling an apology to the class. He said that he was sorry for his actions the previous day, but added one small caveat: he reserved the right once a semester to "blow up." In other words, he excused himself by claiming the right to act unprofessionally as long as it was on a limited basis.

When someone has offended or caused injury to another person, we sometimes hear that they need to "make things right." What is involved in making something "right?" To make it right is to put things back in order or to correct a wrong. It might involve an apology or some kind of restitution. The goal is to try to make it so that there is no evidence that harm was done in the first place. It is to put things back the way they were before any violation or offense took place.

God never acts out of character. He never reserves the right to do anything unseemly. He always treats people as they deserve because both righteousness and justice demand it. If he did not, he would be contradicting his own nature and would therefore cease to be a perfect God. There is never any need for God to make right for something he has done. He

> **There is never any need for God to make right for something he has done. He is never guilty of sin or wrongdoing.**

is never guilty of sin or wrongdoing, so there is no need for him to ever make restitution. However, he does make restitution for errant sinners.

HEADS WILL ROLL

We are well acquainted with instances in the Bible where God punishes sin both immediately and severely. Nadab and Abihu were consumed in a pillar of flame for defying the instruction of God in offering incense (Lev. 10:1-3). Korah and his rebellious supporters were consumed by the earth for the sin of rebellion (Num. 16:1-40). Ananias and his wife Sapphira simply fell dead after lying to the apostles and to the Holy Spirit (Acts 5:1-10). Justice was swift and severe, yet there are cases where sin may never be repaid in the offender's lifetime. Does this mean God is unjust?

We must keep in mind that there are two methods God employs to punish sin. First is a visible punishment. The three situations mentioned previously are of this type. The punishment is apparent to anyone and everyone. There is no question as to the fate of the offender. However, God may also punish invisibly. Some means of punishment are not readily apparent to the human eye. This kind of punishment does not take place in the offender's lifetime on earth in the present. The second type of punishment is located in either the past or the future.

Those who commit evil acts are always given the option to repent. Jeffery Dahmer was convicted and sent to prison for brutally murdering over a dozen young men. He tricked them into getting into his vehicle and drove off, taking them to their doom. He was sentenced to life in prison and was killed by fellow prisoners only a couple of months after his incarceration. He did things that no one would dispute were evil: kidnapping, murder, cannibalism, even keeping parts of his victim's bodies as trophies. But does this mean Dahmer could never repent and enjoy God's grace?

While he was in prison, Curtis Booth, an uncle of my father-in-law, sent

Dahmer a Bible correspondence course. The two corresponded and Booth phoned several ministers until Roy Ratcliff went to see Dahmer in prison. Although skeptical at first, Ratcliff became convinced that Dahmer had truly repented of his crimes. After finally locating a place that could serve as a baptistery, Dahmer was baptized.

If Jeffrey Dahmer's conversion was indeed as true as it seemed, then his sin was already punished. If God truly added him to the body of Christ, then the horrific murders he committed were nailed to the cross. The punishment for those terrible crimes was taken by Christ himself. In an act in history that can only be viewed by the mind's eye, Jesus satisfied the penalty for those crimes by sacrificing himself. There is no reason to think Dahmer will not join the rest of the saved in a glorious eternity.

What of those who do not repent, and who give no evidence of ever being punished in this life? This is a simple question with an equally simple answer. If Christ did not take the punishment for those sins on the cross, then there yet remains a future punishment for them. When the Day of Judgment comes, each person who never truly repented of their sins will have to be punished for those offenses. Otherwise, there would be an eternity full of victims who never had any justice for the crimes committed against them. If this were the case, then there could be no true heaven. Instead, the afterlife would be a nightmarish amalgam of heaven and hell, with both offender and victim standing beside each other in the presence of God. The victims would cry out like the saints, "How long, O Lord?" (Rev. 6:10). The cold and uncaring answer from God would be, "Never."

Why does God require his people to follow his righteous example? Job asked this very kind of question in musing about whether God has been fair with him. In response to Job's inquiry, God responds, "Shall a faultfinder contend with the Almighty? ... Will you even put me in the wrong? Will you condemn me that you may be in the right?" (Job 40:2, 8). We note that God never gives Job the answer he wants, but instead answers with a statement of his divine power. God is the Creator, while Job is the creation. It is not Job's right—nor ours—to question God. As Paul puts it, "Will what is molded say to its molder, 'Why have you made me like this?'" (Rom. 9:20). The answer is painfully simple: we cannot reserve the right to question our maker with impudence.

We should be especially grateful for God's righteousness and justice in light of his omniscience and omnipotence. Without those two attributes, God's righteousness would not be a cause for joy, but disappointment. Think of a God who does not have the power to carry out his justice. He could only tell the offender what he should be doing without any ability to back it up. Or consider a God who was not omniscient. This judge would be no different from any human judge, having to rely on the information gathering ability of others. There are many criminals who have slipped through the fingers of Lady Justice because her agents were unable to gather enough evidence to secure a conviction. A God who was unaware of criminal activity and could not prosecute for lack of eyewitnesses would be a pitiful one indeed.

Even more horrible is the notion of an all-powerful, all-knowing God who is not perfectly righteous. If unrighteousness were behind the creation and maintenance of the universe, what a horrid place this world would be. If God were not perfectly righteous, then he would be capable of unrighteousness. Unlimited power in the hands of an unrighteous God is a terrible thought indeed, for if he ever decided to perform an act of unrighteousness, no one could stop him.

This idea is not all that dissimilar from the Superman movies. In one of the movies, a character played by Richard Pryor finds a way to synthesize kryptonite. But part of the composition is an unknown element. The result is a product that looks like kryptonite, but has a much different effect. Normally kryptonite would kill Superman, but the synthetic production twists him and makes him evil. Superman is supposed to love truth, justice, and the American way, not commit crimes! But who can stop him? No one. Everyone must sit back and accept whatever is in store for them at the hands of the hero-turned-villain.

What would happen if God were fundamentally unrighteous? There would be no restoration possible. Every human being on earth would simply hope and pray (to whom?) that they never got on God's bad side. An unrighteous God would leave no hope anywhere in the universe. No happiness or joy could exist. Life would become not only meaningless, but an exercise in cosmic sadism.

IMITATE ME

Righteousness is conforming to God's standards of goodness. The gods of the ancient Greeks offered no standard. They were guilty of committing all manner of foul acts against one another and against humanity. Their behavior is what one would expect if you could give superpowers to a group of six-year-olds. For the Greeks, morals and ethics were rooted in philosophy, not religion. Religion was little more than observing carefully-designed rituals in order to placate a group of temperamental, narcissistic deities. The philosophers were concerned with right action and proper behavior, how one should treat his fellow man, and what his civic responsibilities were. The gods offered no decent example worthy of emulation.

God is the ultimate standard of goodness. Being perfect, he cannot diverge from that standard. Being righteous, he cannot tolerate others diverging from that standard, either. This fact is on a collision course with some believers today who have a remarkable ability to redefine sin as mistakes, slip-ups, or little problems. We have convinced ourselves that we have the power to mitigate the force of sin without realizing that we have no authority to do so. That standard has already been set by someone higher than us, and we do not have the power to alter it as we see fit.

The avoidance of sin is played out in churches across the world. It reminds me of a story an older friend told me about finding a small cache of pornography under her teenage son's bed many years ago. When he was in his room with some friends, she asked him about the magazines:

MOM: "Hey Jimmy, I found some dirty magazines under your bed."

JIMMY (a.k.a., FIRST CULPRIT): "Uhhh ... magazines? W-what magazines?"

SECOND CULPRIT: "I don't even read magazines!"

THIRD CULPRIT: "What's a magazine?"

MOM: "Well, I didn't think they were yours, so I just threw them away."

JIMMY: "Hmm. That's probably for the best."

Other Culprits nod in thoughtful agreement.

Some are afraid to respond to an invitation because they fear that others in the audience will secretly judge them. Many elderships are afraid to exercise church discipline because they fear reprisal from congregants—or worse, lawsuits. On the other side, many people see church discipline as harsh, offensive, and intolerant. We live in an age of grace, they say. Punishment and censure are a thing of the past for those less enlightened souls who have not embraced the goodness of God. There is no doubt that love and forgiveness of offenses are an integral part of the Christian message, but some have raised it over and above the very important need to realize the righteousness of God.

Even the imagery of the church as the Bride of Christ has elements we would rather it did not. We emphasize the fact that she is presented clean, but forget the fact that she is filthy before her cleansing. She is stinking and dirty before Christ cleans her. The prophet Isaiah uses comparable imagery when he says that even good deeds committed by sinners are like filthy rags before God (Isa. 64:6). This imagery makes us uneasy, and we shift nervously in our seats just a bit when hearing it mentioned in a sermon. It does not fit the image we have constructed for ourselves, an image of perfection and flawlessness befitting the best make-up commercials on television. We have applied what we think is the ultimate concealer, unaware that any concealing taking place is nothing more than self-deception.

The apostle Paul calls us to imitate God. He says, "Therefore be imitators of God" (Eph. 5:1). And while Paul uses the demonstration of love as an example of what it means to imitate God, we could just as easily use it as an example of righteousness and justice. While love means to help others, it also means to love what is lovely, and there is nothing more worthy than the perfect God. Part of God's love is to love goodness and righteousness, to love himself, to love perfection. Since sin is a violation of the good, then the only appropriate reaction to sin is to despise it. Human beings can tolerate it, but God cannot.

Is there a positive side to the justice of God? Actually, yes! God is not only concerned about himself—he is intimately concerned about each one of his people. Every tear shed in pain, every cry in the darkness, every injustice in the night committed in the absence of any witnesses ignites a divine anger that cannot be quenched, cannot be evaded, and cannot be stopped without some kind of punitive satisfaction. There are no miscarriages of divine justice. No sin escapes God's notice, and no crime goes unpunished when the divine court is in session. Injustice does exist in this world, and in abundance—but not in eternity.

QUESTIONS TO CONSIDER

1. What imagery does the word *justice* bring to mind?

2. What would society look like if there were no such thing as justice?

3. Have you ever had to appear before a judge? How did it make you feel?

4. Imagine you are living in ancient Israel. You see people abusing and taking advantage of one another. Injustice abounds. These people are living in a land God gave to them with the requirement that they remain faithful to him. How does it make you feel? How do you think God feels?

5. Is it possible for us to have the same hatred for sin that God does?

6. God's own nature sets the standard for both his and our behavior. In human beings, this would be seen as egotistical and arrogant, if not potentially wicked. How is it different with God?

CHAPTER TEN

JEALOUSY

I f we asked any Christian to name his or her favorite attribute of God, a high percentage of people may respond with love. We could be pretty certain that answers like mercy, goodness, holiness, or righteousness would appear with similar frequency. We know that God is loving, powerful, and holy, so it makes sense to emphasize these wonderful qualities that we ourselves often imitate.

If we were to ask a professor of theology or a graduate student in Bible, they may give immutability as an answer, indicating that the unchangeable character of God gives us complete confidence and surety in his promises. In a world thrown to and fro by the winds of change, we can have absolute certainty that God's unchangeable character is a fortress against the chaos around us.

If we were to survey a hundred people, we can be virtually certain that jealousy would not make the top of anyone's list, perhaps because of the negativity it connotes. Jealousy is often associated with envy, bitterness, and anger. If God is good, how could he possess such a potentially destructive attribute? It should come as no surprise that the attribute of God's divine jealousy would be difficult to come to terms with, much less accept as a good thing.

GOD WITHOUT EQUAL OR GREEN-EYED MONSTER?

Jealousy is almost always described as a negative attribute, something like a combination of fear, uncertainty, frustration, and envy. Yet the Bible describes God as a jealous God (Exod. 20:5). Atheist David Mills points out what he believes is a true contradiction in the Bible when he compares John's statement that "God is love" (1 John 4:8) and Paul's statement that "Love is not jealous" (1 Cor. 13:4) in light of God's own admission.[1]

The Old Testament describes God's jealousy in fearsome terms. Moses warns the people not to forget the terms of the covenant, because God is "a consuming fire, a jealous God" (Deut. 4:24). When instructing the Hebrews about their associations with the people living in Canaan, he tells them, "You shall tear down their altars and break their pillars and cut down their Asherim (for you shall worship no other god, for the LORD, whose name is Jealous, is a jealous God)" (Exod. 34:13-14). Not only does God sound unpleasant; he sounds undesirable—the quintessential bad neighbor.

Paul lists jealousy along with a number of other sins. He tells the churches in Galatia, "Now the works of the flesh are evident: sexual immorality, impurity, sensuality, idolatry, sorcery, enmity, strife, jealousy, fits of anger, rivalries, dissensions, divisions, envy, drunkenness, orgies, and things like these. I warn you, as I warned you before, that those who do such things will not inherit the kingdom of God" (Gal. 5:19-21). How can God still be considered good when Paul admits that jealousy is sinful? Does even God have a dark side?

God's jealousy is frequently misunderstood. One of the most famous examples comes from talk show diva Oprah Winfrey. During one of her shows, she spoke of her changing view of God and its beginning in her twenties. The transformation of her beliefs about God began with what her minister said about God. She said,

---

1.   David Mills, *Atheist Universe: The Thinking Person's Answer to Christian Fundamentalism* (Berkeley, CA: Ulysses Press, 2006), 44.

I will say I was one of those people who used to go to church every—I grew up, as I was sharing with the last caller, you know, in the South and so going to church every Sunday, Sunday School, Baptist Training Union, Wednesday night prayer service, the whole thing, choir, all of it. And when I moved to Baltimore, I was in my 20s, and I remember sitting in a church, you know, one of those big churches where you have to get there at, you know, 6:30 in the morning to line up for 8 o'clock service, and the minister was preaching about—it was a really good preacher—and he was preaching about how God—"the Lord thy God was a jealous God and the Lord thy God would condemn us for whatever," and I remember I—I had a spiritual aha! there. And I was in my late 20s, and I suddenly thought, "How can this God who is all loving and all powerful, why would God be jealous of me?"[2]

Oprah mistakenly assumed that God's jealousy is just like that of human beings: petty, spiteful, and envious. The term often translated as "jealous" is the Hebrew word *qana'*, which means "jealous," but can be translated as "zealous." There are times when the word means "jealousy," as in when Rachel is jealous of the fact that Leah has borne more children (Gen. 30:1) and when Joseph's brothers heard about his dreams (Gen. 37:11). There are also times when God is described as being jealous—or more properly, zealous—for himself or for his people. To put it another way, he has a vested interest in what he prizes most and that interest is invested with emotion.

> **God is jealous because he holds what is righteous in high esteem. God is the only being who can be jealous without sin.**

Many of the references to God's jealousy occur in the context of covenant.

2.   Best Life Series of worldwide webcasts: "Finding Your Spiritual Path," January 14, 2009. Online: http://static.oprah.com/pdf/20090114_sas_transcript.pdf.

That is, somewhere human sin is involved. Since all sin is committed against God, then it becomes clear that God's jealousy is not because he needs or wants something, but it is a response to an offense committed against him. God is jealous because he holds what is righteous in high esteem. God is the only being who can be jealous without sin.

Even with regard to humanity, there are two different uses of the term in Scripture. In writing to the Corinthians the apostle Paul says, "I feel a divine jealousy for you" (2 Cor. 11:2). The apostle is expressing an attitude of protectiveness or watchfulness. His jealousy is a good thing because it is mirroring the divine attribute of jealousy. This is the same sense in which God is depicted as being jealous.

SOMETHING OLD, SOMETHING NEW

When God's jealousy is discussed in Scripture, it often has a connection to the covenant. At Sinai, God establishes with his people a relationship that resembles a marriage. The New Testament imagery of the church as the bride of Christ (Eph. 5:25-27; cf. 2 Cor. 11:1-3) is not new. This image is used in the book of Hosea, but it is found still earlier in how God relates to the people when he makes a covenant with them after the Exodus. The imagery there is very similar to that of marriage in the ancient world. When God leads the people out of Egypt, he stays ahead of them as a pillar of fire at night and a pillar of cloud during the day. It is only after the Sinai covenant that God dwells with his people. This is very much in keeping with marriage customs in the ancient Near East. A husband and wife would be betrothed, which was like marriage except that the couple did not live together. It is only after the marriage ceremony that the two would live together under one roof.

In a sense, the Sinai covenant is like something of a marriage ceremony between God and Israel. Unlike other nations in the ancient Near East, the Hebrews had no concept of a female deity who would be the consort or wife of the male deity. Instead, Israel serves as a kind of wife for God, as we see in the imagery of the first four chapters of Hosea.

Jealousy comes into play when we see the language used for idolatry in the Old Testament. It is usually labeled as adultery. Some of the most famous examples occur in the book of Jeremiah, who roundly condemns the people for their spiritual infidelity:

> The LORD said to me in the days of King Josiah: "Have you seen what she did, that faithless one, Israel, how she went up on every high hill and under every green tree, and there played the whore? And I thought, 'After she has done all this she will return to me,' but she did not return, and her treacherous sister Judah saw it. She saw that for all the adulteries of that faithless one, Israel, I had sent her away with a decree of divorce. Yet her treacherous sister Judah did not fear, but she too went and played the whore. Because she took her whoredom lightly, she polluted the land, committing adultery with stone and tree. Yet for all this her treacherous sister Judah did not return to me with her whole heart, but in pretense, declares the LORD" (Jer. 3:6-10).

The prophet highlights not only the frequency of Israel's infidelity, but also the abundance of her adulterous acts. Scholars see Jeremiah's mention of the "stone and tree" as a reference to the Asherah pole (a wooden pole representing the sacred tree of the Canaanite goddess Asherah) and the standing stones (which represented a group of Canaanite gods). It seemed as if evidence of Israel's idolatry—and spiritual adultery—could be found nearly everywhere.

The connection between God's jealousy and idolatry is quite clear when he tells the Israelites, "You shall tear down their altars and break their pillars and cut down their Asherim (for you shall worship no other god, for the Lord, whose name is Jealous, is a jealous God)" (Exod. 34:13-14). Like the husband whose wife secretly seeks out other lovers, God has every right to insist that his people be faithful—whether it be ancient Israel or today's church.

YOUR HONOR

God occupies a unique place in the universe. He alone is responsible for creating and maintaining this universe. He explicitly states that everything he has done in creation has been for his own honor. Isaiah tells the people that their Lord has elected to withhold punishment from them with the words, "For my own sake, for my own sake, I do it ... My glory I will not give to another" (Isa. 48:11). God does not share his glory with anyone else. What is just as striking about the verse is that God repeats the phrase "for my own sake." Biblical writers emphasized something by repeating it. On this occasion God is emphasizing that what he is doing is for his sake. We may rightly conclude that this is not limited to one instance of mercy, but everything God does. Everything is done for his honor, and rightly so.

Honor was a cherished possession in past times. We might think of the age of chivalry, when swords and pistols would be drawn over the slightest insult to a gentleman, his lady, or his king. Before he was elected President of the United States, Andrew Jackson defended the honor of his wife, Rachel. Before she met Andrew Jackson, she had a previous husband whom she thought had been lost at sea during a great storm. Months went by, and she simply assumed he was dead. In an age devoid of telephone or Internet service, her deduction was a logical one. Sailors disappeared at sea quite often. Thinking herself a widow, she was courted by Jackson, who proposed to her. She accepted, only to find that her husband was very much alive. They quickly got a divorce so that Rachel could remarry.

Charles Dickinson accused Rachel of engaging in polygamy. The whole affair caused quite a scandal, and Jackson tolerated none of it. He challenged Dickinson to a duel at dawn with drawn pistols. The next day, they met at the proposed time. With pistols in hand, they each took ten paces and turned. Dickinson fired first, hitting Jackson in the chest. Jackson returned fire, killing Dickinson instantly. Honor was a precious commodity commanding a higher price than human life.

A challenge to someone's honor was not taken lightly. God would certainly agree, since his jealousy seeks to protect his own honor. God rightfully deserves the worship of every human being, though since humans are sinful creatures who frequently deny his very existence, that level of unified worship will not be realized anywhere in this broken world. God's jealousy also targets those who would ascribe the honor that rightfully belongs to him to another created divine being instead, as with idolatry.

God is indeed worthy of praise. To delight in this fact is to discover the true essence of worship. Praising God does not consist of going to church three times a week, singing some songs, and listening to a preacher or Bible teacher for thirty minutes at a time; it is not punching a spiritual time clock. Anyone who confuses "doing church" with worship is sadly mistaken. Sunday mornings around the world see too few worshippers and too many seat-warmers.

All of creation is like a great symphony, and God intended for creation to honor him (Psa. 19:1-14; Neh. 9:6). Someone without a great interest in the symphony will recognize that there are a great number of instruments playing, but will no doubt have trouble following the intricate patterns of the music. The aficionado will recognize and appreciate the individual instruments. Even the delicate piccolo has a place, as the trained ear knows.

The intricate blessings of life are not unlike a great symphony, though much larger and more complex than any collection of instruments in a great music hall. When we walk outside in the morning, the sun greets us with warmth. We look up to see a beautiful blue sky. We hear birds singing in the background. The flora and fauna of our planet are a never-ending source of fascination and needed resources. Various types of food have unique tastes, and we can exercise our divinely-given ingenuity in creating an endless number of tastes.

We discuss this to make one simple point: God is a craftsman par excellence, and his creation is so intricate and complex that it would take a seasoned philosopher to sit down and appreciate even the smallest bit of what God has given for man to enjoy. A great composer might have a hundred different instruments with which to work, while an artist might have millions of colors. But God works with a creation with such a vast number of different elements that it defies our imaginations. Yet God is still able to number each hair on our head, see to the welfare of each individual sparrow, dress every blade of grass, and clothe every flower on the planet. God deserves the honor he expects to be given, and has a right to be jealous if anything detracts from what rightfully belongs to him.

Like any of God's attributes, jealousy is multi-faceted. God does have the right to be jealous, but when it comes to humanity, his jealousy is actually an expression of concern and care. We might think of it in terms of a child who wants to fritter away his money on candy when he could save it for a bigger, more substantial, longer-lasting prize. We want our children to experience the best, and are disappointed when they fall prey to immaturity and carelessness. More than one parent has experienced exasperation at the shortsightedness of his or her child.

God wants his creation to enjoy the best that life has to offer. Being part of his people is the point of access into realizing the wonders of what he has in store for us not only in this life, but more so in eternity. His anger and jealousy over our own failures is not because he is a Middle-Eastern tyrant demanding our loyalty, but a loving parent who wants us to live the best of all possible lives.

QUESTIONS TO CONSIDER

1. In what ways could God's jealousy make people uncomfortable?

2. How would you describe God's jealousy to a non-believer?

3. Was God's anger over his people's spiritual infidelity justified?

4. Compare Galatians 5:20 with 2 Corinthians 11:2. In what ways might Paul be using the term "jealousy" differently?

5. What is the difference between righteous jealousy and sinful jealousy?

6. What is the relationship between godly jealousy and love? What about between jealousy and commitment?

CHAPTER ELEVEN

WRATH

The wrath of God tends to be a popular topic for discussion in the aftermath of natural disasters and tragic events. In 2005, some labeled hurricane Katrina as God's judgment on the city of New Orleans. September 11, 2001 was said to have been a day of judgment on the entire country. According to some rather misguided televangelists, AIDS was God's judgment on homosexuals. Sometimes we use the same approach in our personal lives. Something goes wrong, and we immediately assume that it is the divine hammer of justice crushing down on us. Even something as small as a bad day at the office, a flat tire, or a 24-hour virus can be blown up to catastrophic, earth-rending proportions in our minds. It is no wonder why some people have an unhealthy fear of God.

In a famous dialogue found in *The Lion, the Witch, and the Wardrobe*, the children who find themselves in the magical world of Narnia get a primer on Aslan. When Mr. Beaver tells them Aslan is a lion,

> "Ooh!" said Susan, "I'd thought he was a man. Is he—quite safe? I shall feel rather nervous about meeting a lion."
>
> "That you will, dearie, and no mistake," said Mrs. Beaver, "if

there's anyone who can appear before Aslan without their knees knocking, they're either braver than most or else silly."

"Then he isn't safe?" said Lucy.

"Safe?" said Mr. Beaver. "Don't you hear what Mrs. Beaver tells you? Who said anything about safe? 'Course he isn't safe. But he's good. He's the King, I tell you."

We know that "God is love" (1 John 4:8). But can he also be a God of wrath? Some would say that the two attributes conflict with one another. Aristotle once said, "One cannot love whom he fears." Can we really love a God we keep at arm's length?

HE IS NO PAPER TIGER

Many Westerners are accustomed to ease. Even the poorest among us lives like a king compared to the rest of the world, and the smallest comforts we take for granted are often considered treasures anywhere else. One of the products of this mindset is user-friendly religion. We want to be comforted; we want to be satisfied. We want our needs met, and if someone is unwilling to do it, we find someone else who will. It is perhaps in response to this mindset that churches have adopted an entertainment style of worship, that preaching centers on felt needs, and that Jesus is reimagined as our cosmic buddy. We dislike negativity, and the less of it we have in our religion, the better.

Because we actively avoid a wrathful God, we tend to make him into a Nice Guy of cosmic proportions. We make nicety, deference, and tolerance the primary attributes of any deity worthy of belief. The only problem is that a God without wrath is a God without teeth. D. Stephen Long puts it this way:

Imagine the extreme makeover this would give Isaiah's vision of God: "...I saw the Lord sitting on a lawn chair, close and friendly; and the emblem of his ballcap said Chicago Cubs [readers should fill in their favorite team name here]. Seraphs...called to one another and said: 'Nice, nice, nice is the Lord of hosts; the whole earth is full of his niceness'" (Isa. 6:1-3, altered a little).[1]

The fact that we do not like a wrathful God is demonstrated in how people approach theological hot button topics. One of those involves salvation. Universalists say everyone is going to heaven. They do not like the idea that a person might be punished eternally for his or her sins. A popular and controversial minister named Rob Bell has said much the same thing in his book *Love Wins*, in which he says that hell is not a place of punishment in the afterlife, but rather the bad choices that people make here on earth during their lifetimes.[2] Like many people, Bell seems to hold a rather dim view of God's wrath.

Many people can and do live with a worldview that sees God as a universal Mr. Milquetoast. They assume that since God is love, he is going to forgive them for sin as long as they show a modicum of repentance. In some ways, it is not even repentance, but rather a recognition that they have perhaps done something unwise. The God of the Bible is not a God who is going to let his creation run roughshod over him. He is holy and just, and in order for that to be possible, God must demonstrate his wrath against sin.

MY, WHAT SHARP TEETH YOU HAVE

God hates those activities that do not conform to his moral character. Sin is the departure from the good, whether it is an action taken or an action forsaken. Wickedness includes not only sins of commission, but also sins of omission. Sin is failure or refusal to conform to God's moral excellence.

Some believe that the "Old Testament God was one of wrath, and the New

---

1.   D. Stephen Long, "God is Not Nice," in *God is Not...: Religious, Nice, "One of Us," an American, a Capitalist.* D. Brent Laytham, ed. (Grand Rapids, MI: Brazos Press, 2004), 41.

2.   For this perspective, see Rob Bell, *Love Wins: A Book About Heaven, Hell, and the Fate of Every Person Who Ever Lived* (New York, NY: HarperOne, 2011).

Testament God is one of love." God did not wake up one morning to realize he had been too harsh with his people and decide to turn over a new leaf. He did not stop to consider that love was so much better than hate and warfare, and that he had actually been wrong all along. The period between the testaments was not a period of enlightenment for God.

The wrath of God is very much present in the New Testament. From no less an authority than Christ himself, the Bible instructs us that "Whoever believes in the Son has eternal life; whoever does not obey the Son shall not see life, but the wrath of God remains on him" (John 3:36). Paul also notes, "For the wrath of God is revealed from heaven against all ungodliness and unrighteousness of men" (Rom. 1:18; cf. 2:5, 8; 5:9; 9:22; Col. 3:6; 21; 1 Thess. 1:10; 2:16; 5:9; Heb. 3:11; Rev. 6:16-17; 19:15). In the eyes of God, all sin is a personal violation of his moral law.

Our reaction to sin tends to be rather underwhelming. Pet peeves will always get a noticeable response, but for many of us, sin generates less attention the farther it is from us. Across the world, people watch countless hours of television full of deceit, theft, and murder, becoming increasingly desensitized to the evils that human beings commit. Unless it happens to us, we often give it little thought.

There was a certain crime show that my wife and I always watched. We watched new episodes on primetime and caught every rerun that showed on cable television. Not only did we watch this particular program, but we also watched its various incarnations in spin-off programs. We had a habit to feed, and we not only feasted, we were gluttons. As it was one of the top-rated programs on television, we knew we were not alone.

One day, I had a turnaround. I noticed that every show featured murder, rape, or any one of a host of other violent crimes. I always knew this on a factual level, but this was the first time it had impacted me on a deeper, spiritual level. The program touted itself as providing stories "ripped from the headlines." These crimes were played in real life thousands of times across the world every day. I had gotten too tired of television villainy to continue watching, but God does not get tired and resign himself to the existence of evil. Each sinful act requires atonement for the One who not only created the universe, but could also destroy it.

WRATH RESTRAINED

Imagine an all-too-common situation: Dad comes home after work to a scenario we will call "the perfect storm." He has had a long day at work, and both his boss and his customers have yelled at him. Other motorists have cut him off on the drive home. Meanwhile, Mom has been keeping a perfect score of every one of the children's behavioral abnormalities. There is a broken vase, frazzled nerves, and weeping and gnashing of teeth. Upon arrival, the bedraggled man is greeted by a now-mentally disturbed wife, shrieking children, and broken furniture—all of which elicits a sudden temptation to turn the family homestead into a crater.

Human beings must always fight the temptation to allow their anger to escalate matters because our anger is nearly always self-interested. If someone cuts us off in traffic, we usually do not get angry because the law has been broken; we are angry because we have been inconvenienced, impinged upon, or endangered by another motorist. There are serious crimes committed every day that do not rouse our anger as quickly as being cut off in traffic. The same goes for virtually every other wrongdoing we might experience. It always seems personal when we have been wronged, but our anger is not worthy of the righteousness of God. His wrath is always a perfectly righteous indignation, and can never be any less.

> **God's wrath is always a perfectly righteous indignation, and can never be any less.**

God's wrath has been feared since Adam and Eve walked in the garden in Eden. God's wrath is often associated with fire and storm in Scripture; however,

Christians do not live in fear of him. Paul writes that Christians "were by nature children of wrath, like the rest of mankind" (Eph. 2:3), and thus subject to God's righteous indignation like every other sinful person. But Christ "delivers us from the wrath to come" (1 Thess. 1:10; cf. Rom. 5:10) so that those who trust in the name of Christ and keep his commandments should not fear God's wrath.

Why do Christians have safety from God's anger? The answer is that Christ satisfied that penalty on the cross on behalf of those who trust in him (Rom. 3:25-26). After having borne the punishment for the redeemed, God cannot justly deliver a second punishment. This would be like punishing two people for the same crime when only one of them should be held responsible. Christ acted as our substitute on the cross, taking the punishment that we deserved.

In Hebrew, anger was described as someone's nose getting hot. We use similar language today when someone gets angry. We might say that a person was "hot about something" or got "hot under the collar." We might also say something like, "He got so mad you could almost see smoke coming out his ears." Like the ancient Hebrews, we connect anger with a rise in temperature.

Having a long nose in the Old Testament is a synonym for patience. If someone is slow to anger, then they are described as being "long of nostrils." English translations do not translate the phrase literally, usually substituting words like *patient* or *gracious*. God is described this way in Psalm 103:8 when the psalmist says, "The LORD is merciful and gracious, slow to anger and abounding in steadfast love." Scripture is clear that God may delay his wrath so that sinful people have more time to repent (cf. Rom. 2:4). However, this does not mean that his wrath is canceled. If God simply forgave sins arbitrarily without any kind of payment, he would be unjust.

HAVING A GOD OF WRATH CAN BE A GOOD THING

Being faced with God's wrath is a fearsome prospect no matter how important a person might be. In 2 Kings 22, priests renovating the temple are shocked to find a copy of the law. When Josiah hears the reading of the law, he rends his clothes in grief. It is not hard to imagine his mounting horror as his secretary, Shaphan, reads one law after another aloud. As each law is read, the king must have been thinking of examples of how each one has been broken by his people. He realizes that he is the king of a nation of criminals.

Facing the wrath of God has led some to engage in a kind of preemptive strike against themselves. The various monastic orders prescribe harsh treatment for the body, in keeping with Paul's statements that he buffeted himself daily (1 Cor. 9:27). Some have gone an extra step, engaging in what they believe to be meritorious self-punishment. Martin Luther felt so guilt-stricken because of his sins that he would confess them every day. When that failed, he beat himself with a whip—sometimes with such ferocity that he would lose consciousness.

Like the jealousy of God, few if any would think that the wrath of God is something to be celebrated, since the idea of wrath carries negative connotations. Even so, we have to ask ourselves, "What kind of God would the Lord be if he did not hate sin and act out against it?" We can see the full importance of God's wrath by putting it into a relational context. Imagine loving someone and discovering that he or she is engaged in sin or a self-destructive behavior. The person knows better and could choose to act differently, but does not. Either he continues to engage in sin, or on the other hand, he refuses to accept help or treatment for his behavior. If we truly love that person, does it not make us angry that the person is destroying himself? God's love works the same way. He sees us destroying our lives and the lives of others through our sin. Anger is not the opposite of love because love involves being angry at anything that harms those we love. The opposite of love is indifference, which is little more than a passive form of hatred.

A God who goes unaffected by sin would be fearsome indeed. He would look down upon the world full of murder, theft, and rape, turning a blind eye to all manner of evil. Thankfully, the God of the Bible has revealed himself as one who utterly hates sin. The prophet Habakkuk praises God that his eyes are too pure to look upon evil (Hab. 1:13). That is to say that God cannot look upon any evil with approval, no matter how great or small. Evil always stirs God's wrath.

God is consistent and does not play favorites. We see this in the early chapters of 1 Samuel. Eli is the elder priest and the next-to-last judge of Israel before the era of the kings. When we are introduced to his sons Hophni and Phinehas, we see two reprobates who are called "worthless men" (1 Sam. 2:12). They abuse their position as priests, snatching the choicest portions of the sacrifices before worshippers can offer them to God. They fornicate with women who serve at the Tent of Meeting. They make public spectacles of themselves, so much that even their father rebukes them.

One night, God calls to Samuel and delivers a message for Eli (1 Sam. 3:10-14). The young man is reluctant to relay the message to Eli because of its grim prediction. Nevertheless, Eli persists and Samuel gives the message. Later on, the outworking of God's wrath sees Hophni, Phinehas, and Eli all dead within a span of hours.

God's wrath is also tempered by justice and fairness. As far as I am concerned, driving is a time of spiritual testing because it seems that my temper is never quicker than when I am on the road. I know that I am not alone in this struggle. A preacher friend once told me a story about getting cut off in traffic by a fellow motorist. He honked his horn at the other driver, who held up an apologetic peace sign. The preacher yelled and shook his fist at the man and, when passing him, realized with horror that the other driver was one of the members of his congregation.

God's wrath does not fly off the handle. We do not ever catch him on a bad day. God's perfection dictates that his wrath is always measured fairly, without prejudice, caprice, or discrimination.

It is important to remember that God may be wrathful, but his wrath is always holy and just. This makes the difference in how a person acts. We might think of it as the difference between how a person acts around his parents and how he acts around the police. We may have loving relationships with our parents when we are children, though we know that we might have to be disciplined. Still, we do not live in fear of our parents as long as they discipline properly. It is a different story when people see the police. Most people slow down well below the speed limit when they see a police car. Sometimes they act a little oddly when they pass an officer on the sidewalk or have to talk to one, even if they have done nothing wrong. The latter is all too common when it comes to our relationship with God.

Reflecting on the wrath of God is vital for our Christian lives. We are able to rejoice because Christ paid for our sins on the cross. We are able to look past injustice in this life because God will ultimately avenge all evil (cf. Rom. 12:19). God's holiness prompts us to live holy lives, and pleasing the Spirit leads to eternal life (Gal. 6:6-7). We fully understand the breadth and depth of God's patience and mercy. It is difficult to fully appreciate heaven without understanding the horror of its alternative. We know that time is short and that those who do not accept Christ will fall under God's judgment. Just as the parent who never disciplines his children will raise kids who are virtually worthless, so God must make his wrath known so that Christians do not live up to the old saying that we "are so heavenly-minded that we are no earthly good."

QUESTIONS TO CONSIDER

1.   What are some common misconceptions about God's wrath?

2.   People in the ancient world feared the wrath of their gods. Why is the wrath of God different than that of others in the ancient world?

3.   Does God enjoy being angry, or are there other reasons why he must demonstrate his wrath?

4.   How difficult is it for you to accept correction from God?

5.   Christians may feel the need to be apologetic or defensive about God's wrath. How can his wrath be a good thing?

6. What is the relationship between God's wrath and his holiness?

7. How often do we think about God's wrath?

8. In your opinion, should God's wrath be mertioned more or less in preaching today?

CHAPTER TWELVE

PERFECTION

God's perfection is an attribute that incorporates all his other attributes. When we began looking at God's attributes, we noted that no single attribute exists in a vacuum. Every attribute has some bearing on all the others. Perfection describes all his other attributes. God is omniscient, knowing everything perfectly. He is also perfectly righteous. His love is perfect, as is his wrath. God can do anything he desires because his power is perfect as well. God never changes his mind or character whimsically because he is perfectly immutable. Of all the words we can use to describe God, *perfect* is certainly one of the best. We might say that he is perfectly perfect.

As human beings, we are inherently limited. Some of us are stronger, faster, smarter, or more gifted than others, but none of us perfectly so. Even the way we speak about God is limited. We try to describe a perfect God, but have to use imperfect language in doing so. All of our language is anthropomorphic in some way. We have to speak about God by relating him to some aspect of our existence. We have to use the closest finite parallel because that is all our limited minds are capable of doing.

For man, the ways of God are far above us (Isa. 55:9). We do not think as he thinks or act as he acts. We cannot, in our limited state, emulate those behaviors of a God who is perfect in every good way. Basic to God's nature is a moral excellence that is incomprehensible to us; we may only say "he is perfect." However, we find ourselves unable to fully plumb the depths of what that statement means (Job 42:3; Eccles. 3:11).

YOU CANNOT STEP INTO THE SAME RIVER TWICE

One way God expresses his perfection is by his immutability, which means, "incapable of change." When applied to God, immutability means that even though he may feel emotions and respond differently to different situations, he cannot change his being (Psa. 93:2; Rom. 1:23), character (Jas. 1:17), promises (Mal. 3:6; cf. Isa. 40:6-8), commands (Psa. 119:89, 151-152), or purposes (1 Sam. 15:29).

After having studied God's omnipotence, we understand that he is completely powerful. The real question is to what extent his power reaches. Since he is the Creator, God can certainly effect change in anything or anyone. His creation is totally subservient to him, doing what he says when he says it. However, if he is the source of all power and can effect change in anything, can he change himself?

The first thing we have to do is understand what it means to change. Early Greek philosophers debated the true nature of reality in exploring this idea. In looking at reality, they were torn between the ideas of permanency and fluctuation. Some philosophers believed that everything was in a state of permanency. The Greek philosopher Parmenides said that everything must be in a state of being. For us to be able to talk about it with any degree of accuracy, it cannot be going through a process of change. It must exist in a fixed state in order for us to know it. Some went so far to say that everything was fixed and all change was illusion.

Others said that all of reality was in a state of change. Heraclitus said that everything mankind knows goes through change. Thus the only permanent thing is change itself. He once said that it is impossible to step into the same river twice. With waters moving and swirling in the current, it would have already changed before the second step could be taken.

It seems that the human experience is defined by alteration and transformation. We are born and grow up. Hopefully during the process of maturing, we will become more educated, more experienced, and develop our skills and talents. Throughout this entire process, we are changing. Accomplishing nothing in a lifetime is often seen as the ultimate waste.

An adult looking back at his childhood knows that the person he has become is quite different from who he was as a youngster. As a general rule, an adult is physically different, more experienced, and more mature. While a person may have the same DNA, the same fingerprints, and the same name, he or she can still undergo a great deal of change in other ways. We can be the same person, yet be quite different at the same time.

In revealing himself to Moses, Yahweh tells him "I am who I am" (Exod. 3:14). Christ also tells the people, "Before Abraham was, I am" (John 8:58). He uses the present tense even though he refers to the past in referring to his own eternality. Unlike his creation, the Lord does not have a beginning or end, so he does not go through the normal processes of degeneration and decay. He cannot become any greater, for he is perfect "as is." As Arthur Pink put it, "He cannot change for the better, for He is already perfect; and being perfect, He cannot change for the worse. Altogether unaffected by anything outside Himself improvement or deterioration is impossible. He is perpetually the same … There is no wrinkle upon the brow of eternity."[1]

There is a sense of discontinuity with the past for created beings. While God sees all of history in a single glance, we experience the present in the moment. It is the future before it arrives, and the past after it has gone by. Change is something inescapable for us. It is simply a part of our nature. This also extends to the realm

---

1.   Arthur W. Pink, *The Attributes of God* (Grand Rapids, MI: Baker Books, 1975), 47.

of non-living things, as in the case of stars that are long gone but so distant that their light remains visible to observers on earth.

PERFECTLY PERFECT

The always-changing nature of humanity has caused some to remark that we should be called human doings or human becomings, rather than human beings. We cannot remain in a perfectly unchanging state, and not all change is good. There are two basic kinds: progress and regress. Progress is movement from the less perfect to the more perfect or change for the better: improvement, advancement, and positive development. Regress is change for the worse, resulting in increasing imperfection or defectiveness: relapse, degeneration, and atrophy.

Change is inevitable for humanity, but not for God. Any change at all would indicate some kind of imperfection. Of all the areas of God's nature and being, perhaps the most important for our discussion is his character. A wide variety of factors can alter a person's character, such as stress, shock, or even a lifetime of experiences. Theologian J. I. Packer notes, "In the course of a human life, tastes and outlook and temper may change radically: a kind, equable person may turn bitter and crotchety; a person of good will may grow cynical and callous. But nothing of this sort happens to the Creator. He never becomes less truthful, or merciful, or just, or good than he used to be. The character of God is today, and always will be, exactly what it was in Bible times."[2] We should also quickly add that God can never be more truthful, merciful, just, or good. He already has those attributes in perfection.

People like redemption stories. We are stunned when our heroes fail, but we cheer them on when they pick themselves back up and atone for their misdeeds. God never has to do that. There is nothing for him to redeem about himself.

For people in the modern world accustomed to the Judeo-Christian world-

2.   J. I. Packer, *Knowing God* (Downers Grove, IL: InterVarsity Press, 1973), 78.

view, the unchangeableness of God is something taken for granted. But the capricious nature of the gods was a fact of life in the ancient world. You could never know when you might catch the gods on a bad day. One classic example is from the *Epic of Gilgamesh*, one of the world's oldest epic poems. In the story, the temperamental goddess Ishtar asks the semi-divine hero Gilgamesh to be her consort. He refuses, citing the fact that her previous lovers have all met untimely ends. She makes promises to him, and then sweetens the deal with a powerful weapon, but still Gilgamesh is unmoved. Even the promises and gifts offered by the goddess are no guarantee that she will keep her word.

Since human beings are imperfect, we often need something to guarantee that another will not go back on their word. In times past, it might have been a simple handshake between friends. For official business, we have more ironclad ways of guaranteeing that we will follow through on our commitments, such as contracts. In the ancient world, they had covenants. These legal agreements guaranteed that the two parties would make good on their promises, usually by invoking blessings for fidelity and curses for failure to keep one's responsibilities. They were witnessed by the gods, who would see through these blessings and curses depending upon the behavior of those making the agreement.

God often makes covenants with people, both individuals and nations. This does not mean that he would fail to follow through on his promises unless he had made a legal agreement to do so. Rather, it seems to have been done to make sure the other party—the one that wasn't perfect—was going to keep their end of the deal. There is no indication in Scripture that God could ever break a promise.

CAN GOD CHANGE HIS MIND?

There is another question about the changeableness of God. Even if he cannot change in his character, purposes, or nature, can he still change his mind? After all, that does not constitute a change in being, but rather a change in action or attitude. Many people assume that he can.

Many would say that it does not diminish God's majesty or power to say that he can change his mind. After all, isn't being willing to change a positive quality? It is, but only for limited or flawed beings. God exists on a higher plane than we do, so there are several reasons why God cannot change his mind (Num. 23:19-20; 1 Sam. 15:29; Psa. 110:4).

First of all, we human beings change our minds because we simply prefer another option at a given time. We might make plans to do something, then change our minds because something else strikes our fancy at that moment. But God's nature is constant and his character is faultless. There is no reason why God should change his mind on a whim. This kind of God would be unpredictable, untrustworthy, and unworthy of worship.

> **God's nature is constant and his character is faultless. There is no reason why God should change his mind on a whim.**

We also change our minds because we become aware of new information. Our plans change because of an alteration in the situation or circumstances. We may make plans to go somewhere, and then be unable to get there for one reason or another. Since there is nothing of which God is not aware, it is absurd to say that we could present new information to God. If he knows everything there is to possibly know, then he cannot change his mind because of something he did not know. Since God knows everything to begin with, it would be illogical for God to make up his mind to do something, knowing that he will later have to change his mind.

A third reason why humans change their minds is because someone forces them to do so. An outside agent imposes its will and forces the person to do something other than what was planned. That person is unable or unwilling to win out, so he or she must change.

Part of the problem we have in understanding this is that God sees all of human history at a single glance. Humans cannot know the past, present, and future simultaneously. We may know the past, but forget it. We may be in the present, but we are ignorant of anything in the universe not within our own perception or experience. We cannot know the future, except for those things foretold by God through his Word. To a very great extent, we are terribly ignorant of the world in which we live.

Even in my short life, I have seen things change, such as the place where I grew up, the university I attended, and the cities in which I have lived. There is a sense of nostalgia that overtakes us when we visit places that have changed. We think back to the times we knew, and we see the old times in a kind of double vision contrasted with what those places look like now. We see the old things, almost like trying to remember a dream we thought we had forgotten. We look upon the past and smile, reminiscing for a moment before it fades away. After those few precious seconds, memory is replaced by reality. We cannot be both places at once because we are bound by time. Either we perceive things as they are now or we close our eyes to remember how things used to be. We cannot do both at once.

Narratives in which God appears to change his mind are often those that deal with the threat of punishment or judgment. God makes it known that judgment is imminent through a spokesman. If the recipient of the message repents, than God's wrath is withheld. If the recipient is not repentant, then God proceeds with the punishment. The person does not talk God out of punishing him. Instead, God is simply withholding the punishment he has promised if that person does not repent. He is exercising his freedom, not changing his mind.

Prophecy has a conditional element, whether it is stated or not. The fact that a prophecy is given and not enforced makes God out to be a liar, unless there are other conditional elements. Even when the outcome is stated, there is an implicit "if." A clear example is that of Jonah and the city of Nineveh. The prophet announces judgment, but because the king and the city were repentant, the judgment was not enforced.

Sometimes what seems to be God changing his mind may actually be a new stage in his plans. God was not surprised when Adam and Eve sinned. More importantly, he did not decide to take one course of action (blessing Adam and Eve) knowing that he would have to change it later (provide a means of atonement for their sin).

God is spoken of as repenting (Gen. 6:6; Jon. 3:10). If there is actually a change in God himself, then he is either changeable or not all-powerful. Many understand these verses to be using anthropomorphic language, describing something not human in human terms. While in Scripture God's plans seem to be unfolding, that is just a human perception. God has always known everything that can and will happen. There is no need for him to take a course of action knowing that it will not succeed or that he will have to alter his plans.

Genesis 6:6 says, "And the LORD regretted that he had made man on the earth, and it grieved him to his heart." The Hebrew term is *naham*, meaning to "be sorry, repent, regret." This word does not mean exactly the same thing for humans as it does for God. When we express regret over something, it is perhaps with the idea that we would have made a different choice if we knew then what we would know later. God feels no need to do this. Just because he makes plans does not mean that he is not grieved when his people fail him. God knows well in advance when we sin, but he is still saddened and angry when it happens.

God is sometimes shown as experiencing pain and regret. For people, these are feelings generated by the tragic unknown. But in relation to God, pain and regret may be understood as anthropomorphisms. These are descriptions of God's actions and feelings from a human perspective. We can only describe them in human language, so they will of necessity be limited to what we can understand.

HIS WORD STANDS FOREVER

In the end, God's perfection should be comforting. He has a moral changelessness that is supremely reliable. We have the assurance that God will never punish arbitrarily, change his mind about the blessings he bestows, or alter his promises. He is perfectly good, eternally trustworthy, and completely reliable. He will always remain so.

His word is eternally true (Psa. 119:89, 151-152) and cannot be annulled by anything (John 10:35). This means that the Word which tells us that God's love is sure (1 John 4:8) and that Christ has made atonement for us and continues to intercede for those who belong to him (Heb. 7:25) will never fail. Scripture is the link connecting us to God until we are able to see him face to face. God does not change and neither does his Word. It is the perfect guide for life on earth until we cross over the threshold of eternity.

QUESTIONS TO CONSIDER

1. In what ways is God superior to the gods found in ancient mythology and other world religions?

2. What are some things that please God?

3. What is God's role in helping us to become increasingly more perfect?

4. Inflexibility or refusal to change one's mind is generally seen as a negative. Why is it a positive when we talk about God?

5. Psalms 18, 31, and 91 all refer to God as a "rock." What does this call to mind?

6. How does God's immutability shape our view of the future?

7. It is often considered a negative for a person not to change, grow, or improve. Why is it a positive with God?

8. If mankind had never sinned, which attributes might God never have had to display?

CHAPTER THIRTEEN

MISUNDERSTOOD GOD

Who is God? For most Christians, this seems like a simple question. It is the God of the Bible, of course! What use is there defining things any further? What else needs to be said?

For an informed Christian or dedicated Bible reader, the identity of God is fairly clear. We understand his greatness and majesty, and we recognize his power in calling the universe into being. We see his knowledge and sovereignty revealed in the unfolding of prophetic announcements through time. We revere his patience with flawed humanity, as well as his love for us at the cross.

For everyone else, the issue may not be so clear. To the spiritual and quasi-religious, he is a force, a spirit, or a vague being whose identity is subject to speculation. To the atheist, he is a figment of man's imagination. To the militant critic, he is public enemy number one. Even those who consider themselves Christians may have some confusion about God's nature and attributes, and we are the poorer for it. As J. I. Packer once said, "Ignorance of God—ignorance both of his ways and of the practice of communion with him—lies at the root of much of the church's weakness today."[1]

All of us have misunderstandings from time to time and will be mistaken more often than we would like. Perhaps the one person misunderstood most often in the world today is God. Who he is, what he does, and why he does it are all areas of interest to theists and non-theists alike, yet people from diverse backgrounds often understand these things very differently.

That someone would misunderstand God and who he is should come as no surprise. This may be the result of simple unfamiliarity with the Bible. This is often the case for non-Christians, especially for militant atheists who seem to enjoy painting God as a cosmic tyrant.[2] It might be that a person simply doesn't know much about the Bible, so his view may be informed more by speculation or hearsay than by Scripture. Another person might come from a divergent tradition—such as a cult or heretical group—in which the biblical text is reinterpreted or distorted. At the heart of these misunderstandings lies the same basic problem: failure to understand the Bible properly.

Christians cannot escape blame, either. Even though we may know the Bible and interpret it accurately, we may have problems of a more practical nature. We cannot deny that many of these problems stem from being forgetful. Why do we worry? We forget that God is all-powerful and that he has everything in control. Why do we resent those who wrong us? We forget about the inescapability of God's justice. Why do we have low self-esteem? We forget that we are wonderfully made in God's image. Each of these problems begins with a combination of forgetfulness and pride. We think that we have to be in control; that we should right the wrongs we suffer; that we have to measure up to someone else's standards. Many of our problems in life would quickly fade if we kept our thoughts focused on God.

While there are a great number of misunderstandings about God we might

---

1.   J. I. Packer, *Knowing God* (Downers Grove, IL: InterVarsity Press, 1973), 12.

2.   See Richard Dawkins' infamous description in *The God Delusion* (New York, NY: Houghton Mifflin, 2006), 51.

examine, we will look at three major source of confusion. These are understanding the misperceptions of: 1) love as sentimentality rather than affection, 2) righteousness as control rather than concern, and 3) perfection as intimidation rather than beauty.

LOVE AS SENTIMENTALITY RATHER THAN AFFECTION

One of the most popular of God's attributes is love. This should come as no surprise. Everyone—except the antisocial, perhaps—wants to be well-liked and held in high esteem. We naturally seek the approval of others and want to experience the joys of friendship and intimacy. It only makes sense that we would want the same from God. "Love," as they say, "makes the world go round."

How the world defines God's love is a different story. Here we find a range of opinions. Some value tolerance, and others value sentimentality. Some seem to want a kind of divine romance with a God who relentlessly pursues them as the object of his affection. Comfort and security rank high on the list of desirable qualities. It seems as if we take what we want in human relationships and simply transfer them to God in the hopes that he will meet our expectations, only on a grander scale. What we may fail to realize is that these expectations are actually quite juvenile. As C. S. Lewis once stated,

> It would seem that Our Lord finds our desires not too strong, but too weak. We are half-hearted creatures, fooling about with drink and sex and ambition when infinite joy is offered us, like an ignorant child who wants to go on making mud pies in a slum because he cannot imagine what is meant by the offer of a holiday at the sea. We are far too easily pleased.[3]

What pleases some people is a saccharine, sentimental love like the kind of-

---

3. C.S. Lewis, *The Weight of Glory and Other Addresses* (New York, NY: HarperOne, 2001), 26.

fered by romance novels and Hallmark Channel movies. This misunderstanding of love creates a wealth of problems. Love without truth is mere sentiment, and sentiment is not concerned with reality. It is cheap and near-sighted. Genuine love wants the others to address their flaws and shortcomings for their own benefit. Sentimentality wants to conveniently ignore such things, to escape from the present reality, rather than build a better one. This is the triumph of dreamy idealism over truth.

On the other hand, sometimes love claims to tell the truth when it is nothing more than cruelty in disguise. We tell others the brutal truth, claiming to care about them; in reality, we do nothing of the sort. We tell them the "truth"—not because we care about them, but because we want to see them change, and usually for our benefit, not theirs. We give them a dose of truth in an act of emotional coercion. We want them to fit our mold, meet our standards, or do things our way. We are nothing if not selfish.

Mere sentiment says, "Don't feel so badly about yourself. You're not as bad as you might think. I love everyone equally. Come as you are." Cold truth says, "You don't deserve my love, and therefore you must do something in order to demonstrate your worthiness. After you have met my conditions, then I will accept you." Notice that here we have two of the most pernicious problems in churches everywhere: far-left liberalism and far-right legalism. Both have chosen a view of love as it might look in a funhouse mirror: warped and distorted. Neither is genuinely concerned for others.

God provides a perfect balance of love and truth. He says, "You are a sinner, and you don't deserve my grace. But because I love you and want you, I am sending my Son as a sacrifice for you." He extends an offer of genuine affection: love for the sake of the other person. After all, we can do nothing for God that he needs and cannot exist without. There is no deed we can perform and no item we can obtain that he must have. Despite the fact that he needs nothing from us, he nevertheless wants our affection while lavishing upon us a divine love that only he can bestow—a love neither sentimental nor cold.

RIGHTEOUSNESS AS CONTROL RATHER THAN CONCERN

If we ranked the attributes of God in order of their importance, we might be tempted to put his qualities of love, goodness, patience, and mercy at the top. Many people do. What many do not stop to consider is that the qualities they deem less desirable—such as holiness, righteousness, and wrath—are just as important.

Imagine a world in which justice and punishment did not exist. Instead, there was only patience, mercy, and forgiveness. For some, this might seem like a utopia, but in some ways it would be a terrible place. Criminals could bargain their way out of trouble by displaying only the mere appearance of contrition. They could commit their crimes with impunity, as forgiveness would spring eternal. Yet victims would remain victims in perpetuity, forever haunted by the wickedness they had suffered with no hope of justice. Humanity itself would be diminished: criminals would never be called to live a higher life of accountability and nobility, and victims would never receive satisfaction for the wrongs they suffered.

The term we know as *righteous* was in Middle English known as *rihtwis*, or *rightwise*. The Hebrew term is *tsedek*, meaning "righteous." It refers to God's quality of being morally right. This is offensive to moderns, who do not like the idea of the kind of absolute standard for right that God provides. We like individual truth and feel oppressed when someone else gets to set the standard without any input from us. Looking at human society, however, we can see the blessing of God's righteousness. It seems that everything we touch becomes tainted with our own imperfection and self-interest.

The Mosaic Law has often been seen as a source of legalism. Proper obedience (read: "lawkeeping") means that a person will win God's acceptance and approval. Failure to maintain strict obedience means that God will judge the individual as a failure at best and reject him or her outright at worst.

It seems that God intended the law to be a source of life. It does not focus purely on external ritual (think of the tenth commandment: "Do not covet"). But a careful reading of the text—and comparing it with other law codes—reveals that the Mosaic Law intended the people of God to achieve a higher standard among the peoples of the world. Other law codes often showed partiality and favoritism toward those who ranked among the social elite. For those on the bottom end of society, justice could be in short supply. Unlike these other nations, God's people were to view others as made in his image, possessing equal worth and value regardless of gender, age, nationality, or social status.

PERFECTION AS INTIMIDATION RATHER THAN BEAUTY

Anything found in a perfect or near-perfect degree of quality will be admired by some and feared by others. The most beautiful woman in the room immediately makes other women feel intimidated or insecure. The fittest guy makes every other male stand a little straighter, pull in his gut, and stick out his chest. We look at someone with a heart of gold who never seems to do anything wrong, and our natural instinct is to feel less worthy in comparison. We see someone with a similar skill set who has attained greater levels of achievement or accomplishment, and we become envious.

We find the superiority or super-competence of other people threatening because we do not want them to make us look bad. No one wants to be outperformed in their job. Students don't like classmates who break the class curve. If we can't be the king of the mountain, we don't want anyone else to be, either.

As the only perfect being in the universe, it should come as no surprise that people would dispute God's perfection. We see it attacked by militant atheists who claim that he is really an evil, cosmic dictator whose character is anything but worthy of imitation. Some theologians describe him as deficient in various ways. One example is a viewpoint known as open theism, which basically asserts that God cannot know the future. Readers in general may see him as a character in a story, one who learns from past mistakes such as the flood of Noah or his disastrous selection of Saul as the first king of Israel. People seem to want a God who is more like them: more human, and therefore less perfect.

God's perfection is intimidating. Humans have responded to it in various ways. We might divide them into three groups. The first are content with their own choices and have little concern for leading a moral life according to Christian principles. This may include the person so opposed to the good that he or she deliberately performs immoral activities in order to offend believers. The second may be moral, but not Christian. They may recognize the need for moral excellence, but members of this group will try to find it in philosophy or other religions. The members of the third group may be moral, and even claim to be Christian, but they have their own ideas about moral perfection and judge others according to that standard because they feel threatened by biblically-faithful Christians.

Each of the three groups views perfection as individually-centered, and perhaps even as a tool or weapon to use against others. They see it as intimidating, perhaps even dangerous. Yet God's perfection is intimidating only for those who are pridefully self-conscious. It is one more of so many reasons why God alone deserves to be worshipped. And though he holds humanity to that standard, we cannot ever forget that he also provides the means through which we can meet it. Though we cannot be perfect, Christ was perfect for us in his life and upon the cross. Ultimately, perfection is something in which Christians may participate.

> **Understanding God is essential for strong Christians and strong churches.**

Understanding God is essential for strong Christians and strong churches. A biblically accurate and robust view of God grants confidence and security, while a diminutive God only offers weakness and uncertainty. Understanding him properly will boost our self-worth and fuel our evangelistic efforts. As the church continues to shine as a bright beacon of light in a darkened world, we must never, ever forget that God is the source of power for that light.

Our neighbors in the world desperately need to know who created them, why they are here on earth, and what eternity has in store for them. Knowing God properly will answer all of those questions handily. Now we must examine our mettle. Do we know him—really know him—and do we care enough to share him with others?

QUESTIONS TO CONSIDER

1. Why is it important to read the Bible carefully?

2. Why would a person misinterpret the Bible when it comes to the portrait of God?

3. In what ways do people misinterpret God to get what they want?

4. How would having a merely sentimental view of God's love impact our understanding of his character?

5. How does a prideful or puritanical view of personal righteousness differ from God's attribute of righteousness?

6. In what way is sentimental love self-centered?

7. In what way is a cold, legalistic love (if it can be called that) also self-centered?

8. Does God's perfection threaten, intimidate, or excite you (perhaps all three)? Why?

9. "When we properly understand God, we better understand ourselves." Do you agree? Why or why not?

BIBLIOGRAPHY

Bell, Rob. *Love Wins: A Book About Heaven, Hell, and the Fate of Every Person Who Ever Lived*. New York, NY: HarperOne, 2011.

Bock, Darrell L. and Gregory J. Herrick. *Jesus in Context: Background Readings for Gospel Study*. Grand Rapids, MI: Baker Academic, 2005.

Bray, Gerald. *The Doctrine of God*. Downers Grove: InterVarsity Press, 1993.

Campbell, Steve. "Boy Fakes Kidnapping to Shed Bad Report Card." *The Huntsville Times*. Online: http://blog.al.com/breaking/2009/09/boy_fakes_kidnapping_to_shed_b.html.

Dawkins, Richard. *The God Delusion*. New York, NY: Houghton Mifflin, 2006.

Lewis, C. S. *The Weight of Glory and Other Addresses*. New York, NY: HarperOne, 2001.

Lewis, Peter. *The Message of the Living God: His Glory, His People, His World*. Downers Grove: InterVarsity Press, 2000.

Long, D. Stephen. "God is Not Nice," in *God is Not...: Religicus, Nice, "One of Us," an American, a Capitalist*. D. Brent Laytham, ed. Grand Rapids, MI: Brazos Press, 2004.

Manton, Thomas. *One Hundred and Ninety Sermons on the Hundred and Nineteenth Psalm, Vol. 2*. London: William Bron, 1845.

Mills, David. *Atheist Universe: The Thinking Person's Answer to Christian Fundamentalism*. Berkeley, CA: Ulysses Press, 2006.

Oswalt, John N. "כָּבֵד" in *Theological Wordbook of the Old Testament*, R. L. Harris, G. L. Archer Jr., & B. K. Waltke, eds. Chicago, IL: Moody Press, 1980.

Otto, Rudolph. *The Idea of the Holy*, 2nd ed. John W. Harvey trans. Oxford: Oxford University Press, 1958.

Packer, J. I. *Knowing God*. Downers Grove, IL: InterVarsity Press, 1973.

Phillps, J. B. *Your God is Too Small*. New York, NY: Touchstone, 1997.

Pink, Arthur W. *The Attributes of God*. Grand Rapids, MI: Baker Books, 1975.

Pink, Arthur. *Gleanings in the Godhead*. Chicago, IL: Moody Press, 1975.

Sanders, John E. *The God Who Risks: A Theology of Divine Providence*, 2nd ed. Downers Grove, IL: InterVarsity Press, 2007.

Sarna, Nahum M. *Exploring Exodus: The Origins of Biblical Israel*. New York: Schocken Books, 1996.

Sproul, R.C. *Truths We Confess: A Layman's Guide to the Westminster Confession of Faith, Vol. 1: The Triune God*. Phillipsburg, NJ: Presbyterian & Reformed, 2006.

Tozer, A. W. *The Attributes of God*. Camp Hill, PA: Christian Publications, 1997.

Tozer, A. W. *The Knowledge of the Holy*. New York, NY: Harper and Row, 1961.

Ware, Bruce A. *Their God is Too Small: Open Theism and the Undermining of Confidence in God*. Wheaton, IL: Crossway, 2003.

Wells, David F. *God in the Wasteland: The Reality of Truth in a World of Fading Dreams*. Grand Rapids, MI: Eerdmans, 1994.

Winfrey, Oprah. "Finding Your Spiritual Path." *Best Life Series of Worldwide Webcasts*. 14 January, 2009. http://static.oprah.com/pdf/20090114_sas_transcript.pdf.

Wright, N. T. *For All God's Worth: True Worship and Calling of the Church*. Grand Rapids: Eerdmans, 1997.

PERSONAL NOTES

PERSONAL NOTES

PERSONAL NOTES

PERSONAL NOTES

PERSONAL NOTES

PERSONAL NOTES

PERSONAL NOTES

PERSONAL NOTES

PERSONAL NOTES

PERSONAL NOTES

PERSONAL NOTES

PERSONAL NOTES

PERSONAL NOTES

Made in the USA
Columbia, SC
21 March 2018